52
VERSES
EVERY
CHRISTIAN
SHOULD KNOW

FAMILY
Christian Stores

Scripture quotations are taken from:

The Holy Bible, King James Version (KJV)

The Holy Bible, New International Version (NIV) Copyright © 1973, 1978, 1984, by International Bible Society. Used by permission of Zondervan Publishing House. All rights reserved.

The Holy Bible, New King James Version (NKJV) Copyright © 1982 by Thomas Nelson, Inc. Used by permission.

Holy Bible, New Living Translation, (NLT) copyright © 1996. Used by permission of Tyndale House Publishers, Inc., Wheaton, Illinois 60189. All rights reserved.

The Message (MSG)- This edition issued by contractual arrangement with NavPress, a division of The Navigators, U.S.A. Originally published by NavPress in English as THE MESSAGE: The Bible in Contemporary Language copyright 2002-2003 by Eugene Peterson. All rights reserved.

New Century Version®. (NCV) Copyright © 1987, 1988, 1991 by Word Publishing, a division of Thomas Nelson, Inc. All rights reserved. Used by permission.

The New American Standard Bible®, (NASB) Copyright © 1960, 1962, 1963, 1968, 1971, 1972, 1973, 1975, 1977, 1995 by The Lockman Foundation. Used by permission.

The Holman Christian Standard Bible™ (HCSB) Copyright © 1999, 2000, 2001 by Holman Bible Publishers. Used by permission.

Cover Design by Kim Russell / Wahoo Designs
Page Layout by Bart Dawsonn

ISBN 978-1-60587-082-3

Printed in the United States of America

52
VERSES
EVERY
CHRISTIAN
SHOULD KNOW

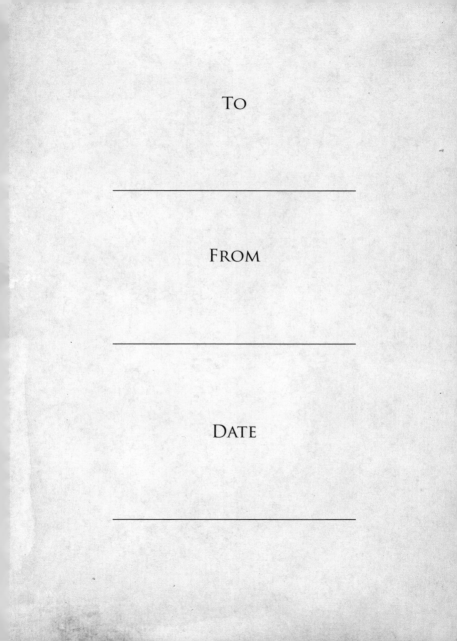

TO

FROM

DATE

INTRODUCTION

There are some Bible verses that are so important, so crucial to the Christian faith, that every believer should know them by heart. Can you memorize 52 of these verses in a year? Of course you can, and of course you should. But please don't try to do it in a week, or even a month. A far better strategy is to study—and memorize— one verse a week for 52 weeks. And that's exactly what this book can help you do. If you just study one verse a week, you'll commit 52 life-altering, spirit-lifting Bible verses to memory. And you'll be richly rewarded for your efforts, both spiritually and emotionally.

This text examines 52 of the most familiar verses from God's Holy Word. These verses, which you've probably heard many times before, are short enough, and memorable enough, for you to place safely in your long-term mental database. So, for the next 52 weeks, read a chapter a week, study that week's verse, and do your best to place it permanently in your mind and in your heart. When you do, you'll discover that having God's Word in your heart is even better than having a Bible on your bookshelf.

TIPS FOR MEMORIZING
BIBLE VERSES

As you memorize each week's Bible verse, here are some things to consider:

1. It helps to write each verse on a note card and carry it with you throughout the week, reviewing the verse often.

2. Memorization is, at its core, the process of moving things from short-term memory into long-term memory. You achieve this through repetition, which means that the more you recite the verse to yourself, the more quickly you'll learn it.

3. Even after you've memorized a particular verse, it's important to review it again and again throughout the year. Otherwise, a verse you've memorized in January may become little more than a foggy recollection by December.

4. Don't be too hard on yourself. If you can't quite master a particular verse, don't quit and don't lose hope. Instead of berating yourself, just keep reciting the verse over and over, until you finally send it into your long-term memory banks.

THE GIFT OF ETERNAL LIFE

VERSE 1

*For God so loved the world,
that he gave his only begotten Son,
that whosoever believeth in him should not perish,
but have everlasting life.*

—

John 3:16 KJV

We begin with John 3:16, a verse that you've undoubtedly known since childhood. After all, this verse is, quite possibly, the most widely recognized sentence in the entire Bible. But even if you memorized this verse many years ago, you still need to make sure it's a verse that you can recite by heart.

John 3:16 makes this promise: If you believe in Jesus, you will live forever with Him in heaven. It's an amazing promise, and it's the cornerstone of the Christian faith.

Eternal life is not an event that begins when you die. Eternal life begins when you invite Jesus into your heart right here on earth. So it's important to remember that God's plans for you are not limited to the ups and downs of everyday life. If you've allowed Jesus to reign over your heart, you've already begun your eternal journey.

As mere mortals, our vision for the future, like our lives here on earth, is limited. God's vision is not burdened by such limitations: His plans extend throughout all eternity.

Let us praise the Creator for His priceless gift, and let us share the Good News with all who cross our paths. We return our Father's love by accepting His grace and by sharing His message and His love. When we do, we are blessed here on earth and throughout all eternity.

MORE GREAT IDEAS ABOUT
ETERNAL LIFE

Teach us to set our hopes on heaven, to hold firmly to the promise of eternal life, so that we can withstand the struggles and storms of this world.

Max Lucado

Your choice to either receive or reject the Lord Jesus Christ will determine where you spend eternity.

Anne Graham Lotz

If you are a believer, your judgment will not determine your eternal destiny. Christ's finished work on Calvary was applied to you the moment you accepted Christ as Savior.

Beth Moore

I can still hardly believe it. I, with shriveled, bent fingers, atrophied muscles, gnarled knees, and no feeling from the shoulders down, will one day have a new body—light, bright and clothed in righteousness—powerful and dazzling.

Joni Eareckson Tada

All that is not eternal is eternally out of date.

C. S. Lewis

The damage done to us on this earth will never find its way into that safe city. We can relax, we can rest, and though some of us can hardly imagine it, we can prepare to feel safe and secure for all of eternity.

Bill Hybels

God has promised us abundance, peace, and eternal life. These treasures are ours for the asking; all we must do is claim them. One of the great mysteries of life is why on earth do so many of us wait so very long to lay claim to God's gifts?

Marie T. Freeman

Like a shadow declining swiftly . . . away . . . like the dew of the morning gone with the heat of the day; like the wind in the treetops, like a wave of the sea, so are our lives on earth when seen in light of eternity.

Ruth Bell Graham

Let us see the victorious Jesus, the conqueror of the tomb, the one who defied death. And let us be reminded that we, too, will be granted the same victory.

Max Lucado

MORE FROM GOD'S WORD

And this is the testimony: God has given us eternal life, and this life is in His Son. The one who has the Son has life. The one who doesn't have the Son of God does not have life.

1 John 5:11-12 HCSB

And this is the will of Him who sent Me, that everyone who sees the Son and believes in Him may have everlasting life; and I will raise him up at the last day.

John 6:40 NKJV

Jesus said to her, "I am the resurrection and the life. The one who believes in Me, even if he dies, will live. Everyone who lives and believes in Me will never die—ever. Do you believe this?"

John 11:25-26 HCSB

In a little while the world will see Me no longer, but you will see Me. Because I live, you will live too.

John 14:19 HCSB

A TIP

God offers you life abundant and life eternal. If you have not accepted His gift, the appropriate moment to do so is now.

WRITE ABOUT IT:
In the space below, write down your thoughts about God's gift of eternal life.

_____

_____

_____

_____

_____

_____

_____

_____

_____

_____

_____

_____

_____

_____

_____

_____

VERSE 2

This is the day which the LORD hath made;
we will rejoice and be glad in it.

—

Psalm 118:24 KJV

Today is a non-renewable resource—once it's gone, it's gone forever. Our responsibility, as thoughtful believers, is to use this day in the service of God's will and in the service of His people. When we do so, we enrich our own lives and the lives of those whom we love.

God has richly blessed us, and He wants you to rejoice in His gifts. That's why this day—and each day that follows—should be a time of prayer and celebration as we consider the Good News of God's free gift: salvation through Jesus Christ.

Oswald Chambers correctly observed, "Joy is the great note all throughout the Bible." E. Stanley Jones echoed that thought when he wrote "Christ and joy go together." But, even the most dedicated Christians can, on occasion, forget to celebrate each day for what it is: a priceless gift from God.

What do you expect from the day ahead? Are you expecting God to do wonderful things, or are you living beneath a cloud of apprehension and doubt? The familiar words of Psalm 118:24 remind us that every day is a cause for celebration. Our duty, as believers, is to rejoice in God's marvelous creation.

Today, celebrate the life that God has given you. Today, put a smile on your face, kind words on your lips, and a song in your heart. Be generous with your praise and free with your encouragement. And then, when you have celebrated life to the fullest, invite your friends to do likewise. After all, this is God's day, and He has given us clear instructions for its use. We are commanded to rejoice and be glad. So, with no further ado, let the celebration begin . . .

MORE GREAT IDEAS ABOUT JOYFUL LIVING

When we truly walk with God throughout our day, life slowly starts to fall into place.

Bill Hybels

If you can forgive the person you were, accept the person you are, and believe in the person you will become, you are headed for joy. So celebrate your life.

Barbara Johnson

When the dream of our heart is one that God has planted there, a strange happiness flows into us. At that moment, all of the spiritual resources of the universe are released to help us. Our praying is then at one with the will of God and becomes a channel for the Creator's purposes for us and our world.

Catherine Marshall

Submit each day to God, knowing that He is God over all your tomorrows.

Kay Arthur

As Christians, we must live a day at a time. No person, no matter how wealthy or gifted, can live two days at a time. God provides for us day by day.

Warren Wiersbe

Today is mine. Tomorrow is none of my business. If I peer anxiously into the fog of the future, I will strain my spiritual eyes so that I will not see clearly what is required of me now.

Elisabeth Elliot

Christ is the secret, the source, the substance, the center, and the circumference of all true and lasting gladness.

Mrs. Charles E. Cowman

Now is the only time worth having because, indeed, it is the only time we have.

C. H. Spurgeon

Yesterday is the tomb of time, and tomorrow is the womb of time. Only now is yours.

R. G. Lee

MORE FROM GOD'S WORD

I must work the works of Him who sent Me while it is day; the night is coming when no one can work.

John 9:4 NKJV

Working together with Him, we also appeal to you: "Don't receive God's grace in vain." For He says: In an acceptable time, I heard you, and in the day of salvation, I helped you. Look, now is the acceptable time; look, now is the day of salvation.

2 Corinthians 6:1-2 HCSB

Therefore, get your minds ready for action, being self-disciplined, and set your hope completely on the grace to be brought to you at the revelation of Jesus Christ.

1 Peter 1:13 HCSB

So teach us to number our days, that we may gain a heart of wisdom.

Psalm 90:12 NKJV

A TIP

Today is a wonderful, one-of-a-kind gift from God. Treat it that way.

WRITE ABOUT IT:
In the space below, write down your thoughts about Psalm 118:24.

_____

_____

_____

_____

_____

_____

_____

_____

_____

_____

_____

_____

_____

_____

_____

_____

_____

_____

_____

VERSE 3

*In the beginning God created
the heavens and the earth.
The earth was without form, and void;
and darkness was on the face of the deep.
And the Spirit of God was hovering
over the face of the waters.
Then God said, "Let there be light";
and there was light.*

—

Genesis 1:1-3 NKJV

In the beginning, God created everything: the things we see and the things we don't. And each morning, the sun rises upon a glorious world that is a physical manifestation of God's infinite power and His infinite love. And yet, because of the incessant demands of everyday life, we're sometimes too busy to notice.

We live in a society filled with more distractions than we can possibly count and more obligations than we can possibly meet. Is it any wonder, then, that we often overlook God's handiwork as we rush from place to place, giving scarcely a single thought to the beauty that surrounds us?

Today, take time to really observe the world around you. Take time to offer a prayer of thanks for the sky above and the beauty that lies beneath it. And take time to ponder the miracle of God's creation. The time you spend celebrating God's wonderful world is always time well spent.

MORE GREAT IDEAS ABOUT GOD'S CREATION

How awesome that the "Word" that was in the beginning, by which and through which God created everything, was—and is—a living Person with a mind, will, emotions, and intellect.

Anne Graham Lotz

No philosophical theory which I have yet come across is a radical improvement on the words of Genesis, that "in the beginning God made Heaven and Earth."

C. S. Lewis

Man was created by God to know and love Him in a permanent, personal relationship.

Anne Graham Lotz

God expresses His love through creation.

Charles Stanley

Because God created the Natural—invented it out of His love and artistry—it demands our reverence.

C. S. Lewis

Big Bang theory—
God spoke and "Bang!"—
It happened.

—

Anonymous

MORE FROM GOD'S WORD

The heavens declare the glory of God; and the firmament shows His handiwork.

Psalm 19:1 NKJV

When I observe Your heavens, the work of Your fingers, the moon and the stars, which You set in place, what is man that You remember him?

Psalm 8:3-4 HCSB

For He looks to the ends of the earth and sees everything under the heavens.

Job 28:24 HCSB

The fool says in his heart, "God does not exist."

Psalm 14:1 HCSB

God saw all that He had made, and it was very good. Evening came, and then morning: the sixth day.

Genesis 1:31 HCSB

A TIP

Every day can be a celebration of God's creation. And every day should be.

Write About It:

In the space below, write down your thoughts
about God's glorious creation.

_____

_____

_____

_____

_____

_____

_____

_____

_____

_____

_____

_____

_____

_____

VERSE 4

After this manner therefore pray ye:
Our Father which art in heaven,
Hallowed be thy name.
Thy kingdom come.
Thy will be done in earth, as it is in heaven.
Give us this day our daily bread.
And forgive us our debts, as we forgive our debtors.
And lead us not into temptation,
but deliver us from evil:
For thine is the kingdom, and the power,
and the glory, for ever. Amen

—

Matthew 6:9-13 KJV

"Our Father which art in heaven, hallowed be thy name." These familiar words begin the Lord's Prayer, a prayer that you've heard on countless occasions. It's the prayer that Jesus taught His followers to pray, and it's a prayer that you probably know by heart.

You already know what the prayer says, but have you thought carefully, and in detail, about exactly what those words mean? Hopefully so. After all, this simple prayer was authored by the Savior of mankind.

Today, take the time to carefully consider each word in this beautiful passage. When you weave the Lord's Prayer into the fabric of your life, you'll soon discover that God's Word and God's Son have the power to change everything, including you.

MORE GREAT IDEAS ABOUT GOD

A sense of deity is inscribed on every heart.

John Calvin

I lived with Indians who made pots out of clay which they used for cooking. Nobody was interested in the pot. Everybody was interested in what was inside. The same clay taken out of the same riverbed, always made in the same design, nothing special about it. Well, I'm a clay pot, and let me not forget it. But, the excellency of the power is of God and not us.

Elisabeth Elliot

God is the beyond in the midst of our life.

Dietrich Bonhoeffer

God is not a supernatural interferer; God is the everlasting portion of his people. When a man born from above begins his new life, he meets God at every turn, hears him in every sound, sleeps at his feet, and wakes to find him there.

Oswald Chambers

It takes all time and eternity to know God.

Oswald Chambers

When all else is gone,
God is left,
and nothing changes Him.

—

Hannah Whitall Smith

MORE FROM GOD'S WORD

Help me, Lord my God; save me according to Your faithful love.

Psalm 109:26 HCSB

The LORD is my strength and song, and He has become my salvation; He is my God, and I will praise Him . . .

Exodus 15:2 NKJV

Peace, peace to you, and peace to your helpers! For your God helps you.

1 Chronicles 12:18 NKJV

Therefore whoever hears these sayings of Mine, and does them, I will liken him to a wise man who built his house on the rock: and the rain descended, the floods came, and the winds blew and beat on that house; and it did not fall, for it was founded on the rock.

Matthew 7:24-25 NKJV

A TIP

If you can recite the Lord's Prayer by heart, congratulations. If you can't, then what are you waiting for?

WRITE ABOUT IT:
In the space below, write down your thoughts about the Lord's Prayer.

_____

_____

_____

_____

_____

_____

_____

_____

_____

_____

_____

_____

_____

_____

_____

_____

_____

_____

_____

VERSE 5

The Lord is my shepherd; I shall not want.
He makes me to lie down in green pastures;
He leads me beside the still waters.
He restores my soul.

—

Psalm 23:1-3 NKJV

David, the author of the 23rd Psalm, realized that God was his shield, his protector, and his salvation. And if we're wise, we realize it, too. After all, God has promised to protect us, and He intends to keep His promise.

In a world filled with dangers and temptations, God is the ultimate armor. In a world filled with misleading messages, God's Word is the ultimate truth. In a world filled with more frustrations than we can count, God's Son offers the ultimate peace.

Will you accept God's peace and wear God's armor against the dangers of our world? Hopefully so—because when you do, you can live courageously, knowing that you possess the supreme protection: God's unfailing love for you.

The world offers no safety nets, but God does. He sent His only begotten Son to offer you the priceless gift of eternal life. And now you are challenged to return God's love by obeying His commandments and honoring His Son.

Sometimes, in the crush of everyday life, God may seem far away, but He is not. God is everywhere you have ever been and everywhere you will ever go. He is with you night and day; He knows your thoughts and your prayers. And, when you earnestly seek His protection, you will find it because He is here—always—waiting patiently for you to reach out to Him.

MORE GREAT IDEAS ABOUT GOD'S PROTECTION

Our responsibility is to feed from Him, to stay close to Him, to follow Him—because sheep easily go astray—so that we eternally experience the protection and companionship of our Great Shepherd the Lord Jesus Christ.

Franklin Graham

He goes before us, follows behind us, and hems us safe inside the realm of His protection.

Beth Moore

The Lord God of heaven and earth, the Almighty Creator of all things, He who holds the universe in His hand as though it were a very little thing, He is your Shepherd, and He has charged Himself with the care and keeping of you, as a shepherd is charged with the care and keeping of his sheep.

Hannah Whitall Smith

The Will of God will never take you where the Grace of God will not protect you.

Anonymous

Kept by His power—that is the only safety.

Oswald Chambers

Prayer is our pathway not only to divine protection, but also to a personal, intimate relationship with God.

Shirley Dobson

God will never let you sink under your circumstances. He always provides a safety net and His love always encircles.

Barbara Johnson

We sometimes fear to bring our troubles to God because we think they must seem small to Him. But, if they are large enough to vex and endanger our welfare, they are large enough to touch His heart of love.

R. A. Torrey

God does not promise to keep us out of the storms and floods, but He does promise to sustain us in the storm, and then bring us out in due time for His glory when the storm has done its work.

Warren Wiersbe

When we hit a tough spot, our tendency is to feel abandoned. In fact, just the opposite is true, for at that moment, we are more than ever the object of God's concern.

Charles Swindoll

MORE FROM GOD'S WORD

I know whom I have believed and am persuaded that He is able to guard what has been entrusted to me until that day.

2 Timothy 1:12 HCSB

For the LORD your God has arrived to live among you. He is a mighty Savior. He will rejoice over you with great gladness. With his love, he will calm all your fears. He will exult over you by singing a happy song.

Zephaniah 3:17 HCSB

In all your ways acknowledge Him, and He shall direct your paths.

Proverbs 3:6 NKJV

Don't worry about your life, what you will eat or what you will drink; or about your body, what you will wear. Isn't life more than food and the body more than clothing?

Matthew 6:25 HCSB

A TIP

Earthly security is an illusion. Your only real security comes from the loving heart of God.

WRITE ABOUT IT:
In the space below, write down your thoughts about the 23rd Psalm.

_____

_____

_____

_____

_____

_____

_____

_____

_____

_____

_____

_____

_____

_____

_____

_____

_____

VERSE 6

But grow in the grace and knowledge
of our Lord and Savior Jesus Christ.
To Him be the glory both now and forever.

—

2 Peter 3:18 NKJV

The words of 2 Peter 3:18 make it clear: spiritual growth is a journey, not a destination. When it comes to your faith, God doesn't intend for you to stand still; He wants you to keep moving and growing. In fact, God's plan for you includes a lifetime of prayer, praise, and spiritual growth.

Many of life's most important lessons are painful to learn. During times of heartbreak and hardship, we must be courageous and we must be patient, knowing that in His own time, God will heal us if we invite Him into our hearts.

Spiritual growth need not take place only in times of adversity. We must seek to grow in our knowledge and love of the Lord every day that we live. In those quiet moments when we open our hearts to God, the One who made us keeps remaking us. He gives us direction, perspective, wisdom, and courage. The appropriate moment to accept those spiritual gifts is the present one.

Are you as mature as you're ever going to be? Hopefully not! When it comes to your faith, God doesn't intend for you to become "fully grown," at least not in this lifetime. In fact, God still has important lessons that He intends to teach you. So ask yourself this: what lesson is God trying to teach me today? And then go about the business of learning it.

MORE GREAT IDEAS ABOUT SPIRITUAL GROWTH

We often become mentally and spiritually barren because we're so busy.

Franklin Graham

If all struggles and sufferings were eliminated, the spirit would no more reach maturity than would the child.

Elisabeth Elliot

We look at our burdens and heavy loads, and we shrink from them. But, if we lift them and bind them about our hearts, they become wings, and on them we can rise and soar toward God.

Mrs. Charles E. Cowman

We set our eyes on the finish line, forgetting the past, and straining toward the mark of spiritual maturity and fruitfulness.

Vonette Bright

The vigor of our spiritual lives will be in exact proportion to the place held by the Bible in our lives and in our thoughts.

George Mueller

Grow, dear friends, but grow, I beseech you, in God's way, which is the only true way.

Hannah Whitall Smith

You are either becoming more like Christ every day or you're becoming less like Him. There is no neutral position in the Lord.

Stormie Omartian

God's plan for our guidance is for us to grow gradually in wisdom before we get to the crossroads.

Bill Hybels

We are either the masters or the victims of our attitudes. It is a matter of personal choice. Who we are today is the result of choices we made yesterday. Tomorrow, we will become what we choose today. To change means to choose to change.

John Maxwell

A person who gazes and keeps on gazing at Jesus becomes like him in appearance.

E. Stanley Jones

MORE FROM GOD'S WORD

For this reason also, since the day we heard this, we haven't stopped praying for you. We are asking that you may be filled with the knowledge of His will in all wisdom and spiritual understanding.

Colossians 1:9 HCSB

I want their hearts to be encouraged and joined together in love, so that they may have all the riches of assured understanding, and have the knowledge of God's mystery—Christ.

Colossians 2:2 HCSB

Therefore, leaving the elementary message about the Messiah, let us go on to maturity.

Hebrews 6:1 HCSB

Now may the God of hope fill you with all joy and peace in believing, so that you may overflow with hope by the power of the Holy Spirit.

Romans 15:13 HCSB

A TIP

Wherever you are in your spiritual journey, it's always the right time to take another step toward God.

WRITE ABOUT IT:
In the space below, write down your thoughts about your own spiritual growth.

_____

_____

_____

_____

_____

_____

_____

_____

_____

_____

_____

_____

_____

_____

_____

_____

_____

_____

VERSE 7

But those who wait on the Lord
shall renew their strength;
They shall mount up with wings like eagles,
They shall run and not be weary,
They shall walk and not faint.

—

Isaiah 40:31 NKJV

Even the most inspired Christians can, from time to time, find themselves running on empty. The demands of daily life can drain us of our strength and rob us of the joy that is rightfully ours in Christ. When we find ourselves tired, discouraged, or worse, there is a source from whom we can draw the power needed to recharge our spiritual batteries. That source is God.

God intends that His children lead joyous lives filled with abundance and peace. But sometimes, abundance and peace seem very far away. It is then that we must turn to God for renewal, and when we do, He will restore us if we allow Him to do so.

Today, like every other day, is literally brimming with possibilities. Whether we realize it or not, God is always working in us and through us; our job is to let Him do His work without undue interference. Yet we are imperfect beings who, because of our limited vision, often resist God's will. And oftentimes, because of our stubborn insistence on squeezing too many activities into a 24-hour day, we allow ourselves to become exhausted, or frustrated, or both.

Are you tired or troubled? Turn your heart toward God in prayer. Are you weak or worried? Take the time—or, more accurately, make the time—to delve deeply into God's Holy Word. Are you spiritually depleted? Call upon fellow believers to support you, and call upon Christ to renew your spirit and your life. Are you simply overwhelmed by the demands of the day? Pray for the wisdom to simplify your life. Are you exhausted? Pray for the wisdom to rest a little more and worry a little less.

When you do these things, you'll discover that the Creator of the universe stands always ready and always able to create a new sense of wonderment and joy in you.

MORE GREAT IDEAS ABOUT STRENGTH

The same God who empowered Samson, Gideon, and Paul seeks to empower my life and your life, because God hasn't changed.

Bill Hybels

No matter how heavy the burden, daily strength is given, so I expect we need not give ourselves any concern as to what the outcome will be. We must simply go forward.

Annie Armstrong

When we spend time with Christ, He supplies us with strength and encourages us in the pursuit of His ways.

Elizabeth George

Worry does not empty tomorrow of its sorrow; it empties today of its strength.

Corrie ten Boom

God conquers only what we yield to Him. Yet, when He does, and when our surrender is complete, He fills us with a new strength that we could never have known by ourselves. His conquest is our victory!

Shirley Dobson

A divine strength is given to those who yield themselves to the Father and obey what He tells them to do.

Warren Wiersbe

When the dream of our heart is one that God has planted there, a strange happiness flows into us. At that moment, all of the spiritual resources of the universe are released to help us. Our praying is then at one with the will of God and becomes a channel for the Creator's purposes for us and our world.

Catherine Marshall

If we take God's program, we can have God's power—not otherwise.

E. Stanley Jones

One reason so much American Christianity is a mile wide and an inch deep is that Christians are simply tired. Sometimes you need to kick back and rest for Jesus' sake.

Dennis Swanberg

MORE FROM GOD'S WORD

And He said to me, "My grace is sufficient for you, for My strength is made perfect in weakness."

2 Corinthians 12:9 NKJV

You, therefore, my child, be strong in the grace that is in Christ Jesus.

2 Timothy 2:1 HCSB

The Lord is my strength and my song; He has become my salvation.

Exodus 15:2 HCSB

Finally, be strengthened by the Lord and by His vast strength.

Ephesians 6:10 HCSB

A TIP

When you are tired, fearful, or discouraged, God can restore your strength.

WRITE ABOUT IT:
In the space below, write down your thoughts about Isaiah 40:31.

_____

_____

_____

_____

_____

_____

_____

_____

_____

_____

_____

_____

_____

_____

_____

_____

BE STILL

VERSE 8

Be still, and know that I am God . . . .

—

Psalm 46:10 KJV

We live in a noisy world, a world filled with distractions, frustrations, obligations, and complications. But we must not allow our clamorous world to separate us from God's peace. Instead, we must "be still" so that we might sense the presence of God.

If we are to maintain righteous minds and compassionate hearts, we must take time each day for prayer and for meditation. We must make ourselves still in the presence of our Creator. We must quiet our minds and our hearts so that we might sense God's love, God's will, and God's Son.

Has the busy pace of life robbed you of the peace that might otherwise be yours through Jesus Christ? If so, it's time to reorder your priorities. Nothing is more important than the time you spend with your Savior. So be still and claim the inner peace that is your spiritual birthright: the peace of Jesus Christ. It is offered freely; it has been paid for in full; it is yours for the asking. So ask. And then share.

MORE GREAT IDEAS ABOUT QUIET TIME

Since the quiet hour spent with God is the preacher's power-house, the devil centers his attention on that source of strength.

Vance Havner

The manifold rewards of a serious, consistent prayer life demonstrate clearly that time with our Lord should be our first priority.

Shirley Dobson

I don't see how any Christian can survive, let alone live life as more than a conqueror, apart from a quiet time alone with God.

Kay Arthur

The Lord Jesus, available to people much of the time, left them, sometimes a great while before day, to go up to the hills where He could commune in solitude with His Father.

Elisabeth Elliot

In the center of a hurricane there is absolute quiet and peace. There is no safer place than in the center of the will of God.

Corrie ten Boom

When we are in the presence of God, removed from distractions, we are able to hear him more clearly, and a secure environment has been established for the young and broken places in our hearts to surface.

John Eldredge

When frustrations develop into problems that stress you out, the best way to cope is to stop, catch your breath, and do something for yourself, not out of selfishness, but out of wisdom.

Barbara Johnson

That is the source of Jeremiah's living persistence, his creative constancy. He was up before the sun, listening to God's word. Rising early, he was quiet and attentive before his Lord. Long before the yelling started, the mocking, the complaining, there was this centering, discovering, exploring time with God.

Eugene Peterson

Quiet time is giving God your undivided attention for a predetermined amount of time for the purpose of talking to and hearing from Him.

Charles Stanley

MORE FROM GOD'S WORD

In quietness and trust is your strength.

Isaiah 30:15 NASB

Be silent before the Lord and wait expectantly for Him.

Psalm 37:7 HCSB

The one who is from God listens to God's words. This is why you don't listen, because you are not from God.

John 8:47 HCSB

Consider it a great joy, my brothers, whenever you experience various trials, knowing that the testing of your faith produces endurance. But endurance must do its complete work, so that you may be mature and complete, lacking nothing.

James 1:2-4 HCSB

A TIP

Be still and listen to God. He has something important to say to you.

Write About It:
In the space below, write down your thoughts about Psalm 46:10.

_____

_____

_____

_____

_____

_____

_____

_____

_____

_____

_____

_____

_____

_____

_____

_____

THE GREATEST OF THESE IS LOVE

VERSE 9

And now abide faith, hope, love, these three;
but the greatest of these is love.

—

1 Corinthians 13:13 NKJV

The familiar words of 1st Corinthians 13 remind us of the importance of love. Faith is important, of course. So, too, is hope. But love is more important still.

Christ showed His love for us on the cross, and, as Christians, we are called upon to return Christ's love by sharing it. We are commanded (not advised, not encouraged . . . commanded!) to love one another just as Christ loved us (John 13:34). That's a tall order, but as Christians, we are obligated to follow it.

Sometimes love is easy (puppies and sleeping children come to mind), and sometimes love is hard (fallible human beings come to mind). But God's Word is clear: We are to love all our friends and neighbors, not just the lovable ones. So today, take time to spread Christ's message by word and by example. And the greatest of these, of course, is example.

MORE GREAT IDEAS ABOUT LOVE

He who is filled with love is filled with God Himself.

St. Augustine

Those who abandon ship the first time it enters a storm miss the calm beyond. And the rougher the storms weathered together, the deeper and stronger real love grows.

Ruth Bell Graham

Love is an attribute of God. To love others is evidence of a genuine faith.

Kay Arthur

Love is the seed of all hope. It is the enticement to trust, to risk, to try, and to go on.

Gloria Gaither

How much a person loves someone is obvious by how much he is willing to sacrifice for that person.

Bill Bright

It is when we come to the Lord in our nothingness, our powerlessness and our helplessness that He then enables us to love in a way which, without Him, would be absolutely impossible.

Elisabeth Elliot

Live your lives in love, the same sort of love which Christ gives us, and which He perfectly expressed when He gave Himself as a sacrifice to God.

Corrie ten Boom

Suppose that I understand the Bible. And, suppose that I am the greatest preacher who ever lived! The Apostle Paul wrote that unless I have love, "I am nothing."

Billy Graham

Carve your name on hearts, not on marble.

C. H. Spurgeon

How do you spell love? When you reach the point where the happiness, security, and development of another person is as much of a driving force to you as your own happiness, security, and development, then you have a mature love. True love is spelled G-I-V-E. It is not based on what you can get, but rooted in what you can give to the other person.

Josh McDowell

MORE FROM GOD'S WORD

Beloved, if God so loved us, we also ought to love one another.

1 John 4:11 NASB

The one who loves his brother remains in the light, and there is no cause for stumbling in him.

1 John 2:10 HCSB

Now these three remain: faith, hope, and love. But the greatest of these is love.

1 Corinthians 13:13 HCSB

No one has ever seen God. If we love one another, God remains in us and His love is perfected in us.

1 John 4:12 HCSB

And we have this command from Him: the one who loves God must also love his brother.

1 John 4:21 HCSB

A TIP

God is love, and He expects you to share His love with others.

WRITE ABOUT IT:
In the space below, write down your thoughts about 1 Corinthians 13:13.

BEYOND WORRY

VERSE 10

*But seek first the kingdom of God
and His righteousness,
and all these things shall be added to you.
Therefore do not worry about tomorrow,
for tomorrow will worry about its own things.
Sufficient for the day is its own trouble.*

—

Matthew 6:33-34 NKJV

Because we are imperfect human beings struggling with imperfect circumstances, we worry. Even though we, as Christians, have the assurance of salvation—even though we, as Christians, have the promise of God's love and protection—we find ourselves fretting over the inevitable frustrations of everyday life. Jesus understood our concerns when He spoke the reassuring words found in the 6th chapter of Matthew.

Where is the best place to take your worries? Take them to God. Take your troubles to Him; take your fears to Him; take your doubts to Him; take your weaknesses to Him; take your sorrows to Him . . . and leave them all there. Seek protection from the One who offers you eternal salvation; build your spiritual house upon the Rock that cannot be moved.

Perhaps you are concerned about your future, your health, or your finances. Or perhaps you are simply a "worrier" by nature. If so, make Matthew 6 a regular part of your daily Bible reading. This beautiful passage will remind you that God still sits in His heaven and you are His beloved child. Then, perhaps, you will worry a little less and trust God a little more, and that's as it should be because God is trustworthy . . . and you are protected.

MORE GREAT IDEAS ABOUT WORRY

The beginning of anxiety is the end of faith, and the beginning of true faith is the end of anxiety.

George Mueller

Worry is the senseless process of cluttering up tomorrow's opportunities with leftover problems from today.

Barbara Johnson

Never yield to gloomy anticipation. Place your hope and confidence in God. He has no record of failure.

Mrs. Charles E. Cowman

We are not called to be burden-bearers, but cross-bearers and light-bearers. We must cast our burdens on the Lord.

Corrie ten Boom

God is bigger than your problems. Whatever worries press upon you today, put them in God's hands and leave them there.

Billy Graham

Today is the tomorrow we worried about yesterday.

Dennis Swanberg

This life of faith, then, consists in just this—being a child in the Father's house. Let the ways of childish confidence and freedom from care, which so please you and win your heart when you observe your own little ones, teach you what you should be in your attitude toward God.

Hannah Whitall Smith

Today is mine. Tomorrow is none of my business. If I peer anxiously into the fog of the future, I will strain my spiritual eyes so that I will not see clearly what is required of me now.

Elisabeth Elliott

Worry and anxiety are sand in the machinery of life; faith is the oil.

E. Stanley Jones

Much that worries us beforehand can, quite unexpectedly, have a happy and simple solution. Worries just don't matter. Things really are in a better hand than ours.

Dietrich Bonhoeffer

MORE FROM GOD'S WORD

Those who trust in the Lord are like Mount Zion. It cannot be shaken; it remains forever.

Psalm 125:1 HCSB

Don't worry about anything, but in everything, through prayer and petition with thanksgiving, let your requests be made known to God.

Philippians 4:6 HCSB

Your heart must not be troubled. Believe in God; believe also in Me.

John 14:1 HCSB

Come to Me, all you who labor and are heavy laden, and I will give you rest. Take My yoke upon you and learn from Me, for I am gentle and lowly in heart, and you will find rest for your souls. For My yoke is easy and My burden is light.

Matthew 11:28-30 NKJV

A TIP

Work hard, pray harder, and if you have any worries, take them to God—and leave them there.

WRITE ABOUT IT:

In the space below, write down your thoughts about God's ability to handle your problems.

_____

_____

_____

_____

_____

_____

_____

_____

_____

_____

_____

_____

_____

_____

_____

_____

_____

TRUST HIM

VERSE 11

Trust in the Lord with all your heart,
and lean not on your own understanding;
In all your ways acknowledge Him,
and He shall direct your paths.

—

Proverbs 3:5-6 NKJV

It's easy to talk about trusting God, but when it comes to actually trusting Him, that's considerably harder. Why? Because genuine trust in God requires more than words; it requires a willingness to follow God's lead and a willingness to obey His commandments. (These, by the way, are not easy things to do.)

Have you spent more time talking about Christ than walking in His footsteps? If so, God wants to have a little chat with you. And, if you're unwilling to talk to Him, He may take other actions in order to grab your attention.

Thankfully, whenever you're willing to talk with God, He's willing to listen. And, the instant that you decide to place Him squarely in the center of your life, He will respond to that decision with blessings that are too unexpected to predict and too numerous to count.

The next time you find your courage tested to the limit, lean upon God's promises. Trust His Son. Remember that God is always near and that He is your protector and your deliverer. When you are worried, anxious, or afraid, call upon Him. God can handle your troubles infinitely better than you can, so turn them over to Him. Remember that God rules both mountaintops and valleys—with limitless wisdom and love—now and forever.

MORE GREAT IDEAS ABOUT TRUSTING GOD

God is God. He knows what he is doing. When you can't trace his hand, trust his heart.

Max Lucado

Sometimes the very essence of faith is trusting God in the midst of things He knows good and well we cannot comprehend.

Beth Moore

A prayerful heart and an obedient heart will learn, very slowly and not without sorrow, to stake everything on God Himself.

Elisabeth Elliot

Do not be afraid, then, that if you trust, or tell others to trust, the matter will end there. Trust is only the beginning and the continual foundation. When we trust Him, the Lord works, and His work is the important part of the whole matter.

Hannah Whitall Smith

Beware of trusting in yourself, and see that you trust in the Lord.

Oswald Chambers

Faith does not eliminate problems. Faith keeps you in a trusting relationship with God in the midst of your problems.

Henry Blackaby

Brother, is your faith looking upward today? / Trust in the promise of the Savior. / Sister, is the light shining bright on your way? / Trust in the promise of thy Lord.

Fanny Crosby

Are you serious about wanting God's guidance to become the person he wants you to be? The first step is to tell God that you know you can't manage your own life; that you need his help.

Catherine Marshall

The hope we have in Jesus is the anchor for the soul—something sure and steadfast, preventing drifting or giving way, lowered to the depth of God's love.

Franklin Graham

Trustfulness is based on confidence in God whose ways I do not understand.

Oswald Chambers

MORE FROM GOD'S WORD

Let us hold fast the confession of our hope without wavering, for He who promised is faithful.

Hebrews 10:23 NKJV

Lord, I turn my hope to You. My God, I trust in You. Do not let me be disgraced; do not let my enemies gloat over me.

Psalm 25:1-2 HCSB

He granted their request because they trusted in Him.

1 Chronicles 5:20 HCSB

The one who understands a matter finds success, and the one who trusts in the Lord will be happy.

Proverbs 16:20 HCSB

Thanks be to God for His indescribable gift.

2 Corinthians 9:15 HCSB

A TIP

Because God is trustworthy—and because He has made promises to you that He intends to keep—you are protected.

WRITE ABOUT IT:
In the space below, write down your thoughts about Proverbs 3:5-6.

_____

_____

_____

_____

_____

_____

_____

_____

_____

_____

_____

_____

_____

_____

_____

_____

_____

VERSE 12

I am the vine, you are the branches.
He who abides in Me, and I in him,
bears much fruit;
for without Me you can do nothing.

—

John 15:5 NKJV

He was the Son of God, but He wore a crown of thorns. He was the Savior of mankind, yet He was put to death on a roughhewn cross. He offered His healing touch to an unsaved world, and yet the same hands that had healed the sick and raised the dead were pierced with nails.

Jesus Christ, the Son of God, was born into humble circumstances. He walked this earth, not as a ruler of men, but as the Savior of mankind. His crucifixion, a torturous punishment that was intended to end His life and His reign, instead became the pivotal event in the history of all humanity. Christ sacrificed His life on the cross so that we might have eternal life. This gift, freely given by God's only begotten Son, is the priceless possession of everyone who accepts Him as Lord and Savior.

Why did Christ endure the humiliation and torture of the cross? He did it for you. His love is as near as your next breath, as personal as your next thought, more essential than your next heartbeat. And what must you do in response to the Savior's gifts? You must accept His love, praise His name, and share His message of salvation. And, you must conduct yourself in a manner that demonstrates to all the world that your acquaintance with the Master is not a passing fancy but that it is, instead, the cornerstone and the touchstone of your life.

MORE GREAT IDEAS ABOUT JESUS

Jesus was the perfect reflection of God's nature in every situation He encountered during His time here on earth.

Bill Hybels

Jesus makes God visible. But that truth does not make Him somehow less than God. He is equally supreme with God.

Anne Graham Lotz

Tell me the story of Jesus. Write on my heart every word. Tell me the story most precious, sweetest that ever was heard.

Fanny Crosby

The crucial question for each of us is this: What do you think of Jesus, and do you yet have a personal acquaintance with Him?

Hannah Whitall Smith

Had Jesus been the Word become word, He would have spun theories about life, but since he was the Word become flesh, he put shoes on all his theories and made them walk.

E. Stanley Jones

Sold for thirty pieces of silver, he redeemed the world.

R. G. Lee

Christians see sin for what it is: willful rebellion against the rulership of God in their lives. And in turning from their sin, they have embraced God's only means of dealing with sin: Jesus.

Kay Arthur

In your greatest weakness, turn to your greatest strength, Jesus, and hear Him say, "My grace is sufficient for you, for My strength is made perfect in weakness" (2 Corinthians 12:9, NKJV).

Lisa Whelchel

There is not a single thing that Jesus cannot change, control, and conquer because He is the living Lord.

Franklin Graham

When you can't see him, trust him. Jesus is closer than you ever dreamed.

Max Lucado

MORE FROM GOD'S WORD

I am the door. If anyone enters by Me, he will be saved.

John 10:9 NKJV

I have come as a light into the world, so that everyone who believes in Me would not remain in darkness.

John 12:46 HCSB

We have seen it and we testify and declare to you the eternal life that was with the Father and was revealed to us—what we have seen and heard we also declare to you, so that you may have fellowship along with us; and indeed our fellowship is with the Father and with His Son Jesus Christ.

1 John 1:2-4 HCSB

But we do see Jesus—made lower than the angels for a short time so that by God's grace He might taste death for everyone— crowned with glory and honor because of the suffering of death.

Hebrews 2:9 HCSB

A TIP

Jesus is the light of the world. God wants Him to be the light of your life.

WRITE ABOUT IT:
In the space below, write down your thoughts about John 15:5.

_____

_____

_____

_____

_____

_____

_____

_____

_____

_____

_____

_____

_____

_____

_____

_____

_____

_____

ASK HIM FOR THE THINGS YOU NEED

VERSE 13

Ask, and it will be given to you;
seek, and you will find;
knock, and it will be opened to you.
For everyone who asks receives,
and he who seeks finds,
and to him who knocks it will be opened.

—

Matthew 7:7-8 NKJV

How often do you ask God for His help and His wisdom? Occasionally? Intermittently? Whenever you experience a crisis? Hopefully not. Hopefully, you've acquired the habit of asking for God's assistance early and often. And hopefully, you have learned to seek His guidance in every aspect of your life.

In Matthew 7, God promises that He will guide you if you let Him. Your job is to let Him. But sometimes, you will be tempted to do otherwise. Sometimes, you'll be tempted to go along with the crowd; other times, you'll be tempted to do things your way, not God's way. When you feel those temptations, resist them.

God has promised that when you ask for His help, He will not withhold it. So ask. Ask Him to meet the needs of your day. Ask Him to lead you, to protect you, and to correct you. And trust the answers He gives.

God stands at the door and waits. When you knock, He opens. When you ask, He answers. Your task, of course, is to seek His guidance prayerfully, confidently, and often.

MORE GREAT IDEAS ABOUT ASKING GOD

All we have to do is to acknowledge our need, move from self-sufficiency to dependence, and ask God to become our hiding place.

Bill Hybels

By asking in Jesus' name, we're making a request not only in His authority, but also for His interests and His benefit.

Shirley Dobson

When will we realize that we're not troubling God with our questions and concerns? His heart is open to hear us—his touch nearer than our next thought—as if no one in the world existed but us. Our very personal God wants to hear from us personally.

Gigi Graham Tchividjian

God uses our most stumbling, faltering faith-steps as the open door to His doing for us "more than we ask or think."

Catherine Marshall

Some people think God does not like to be troubled with our constant asking. But, the way to trouble God is not to come at all.

D. L. Moody

Often I have made a request of God with earnest pleadings even backed up with Scripture, only to have Him say "No" because He had something better in store.

Ruth Bell Graham

God makes prayer as easy as possible for us. He's completely approachable and available, and He'll never mock or upbraid us for bringing our needs before Him.

Shirley Dobson

Don't be afraid to ask your heavenly Father for anything you need. Indeed, nothing is too small for God's attention or too great for his power.

Dennis Swanberg

Notice that we must ask. And we will sometimes struggle to hear and struggle with what we hear. But personally, it's worth it. I'm after the path of life—and he alone knows it.

John Eldredge

God's help is always available, but it is only given to those who seek it.

Max Lucado

MORE FROM GOD'S WORD

Don't worry about anything, but in everything, through prayer and petition with thanksgiving, let your requests be made known to God.

Philippians 4:6 HCSB

What father among you, if his son asks for a fish, will, instead of a fish, give him a snake? Or if he asks for an egg, will give him a scorpion? If you then, who are evil, know how to give good gifts to your children, how much more will the heavenly Father give the Holy Spirit to those who ask Him?

Luke 11:11-13 HCSB

So I say to you, keep asking, and it will be given to you. Keep searching, and you will find. Keep knocking, and the door will be opened to you.

Luke 11:9 HCSB

You do not have because you do not ask.

James 4:2 HCSB

A TIP

If you sincerely want to guard your steps, ask for God's help.

WRITE ABOUT IT:
In the space below, write down your thoughts
about Matthew 7:7-8.

_____

_____

_____

_____

_____

_____

_____

_____

_____

_____

_____

_____

_____

_____

_____

_____

_____

PUTTING GOD FIRST

VERSE 14

You shall have no other gods before Me.

—

Exodus 20:3 NKJV

I s God your top priority? Have you given His Son your heart, your soul, your talents, and your time? Or are you in the habit of giving God little more than a few hours on Sunday morning? The answers to these questions will determine how you prioritize your days and your life.

As you contemplate your own relationship with God, remember this: all of mankind is engaged in the practice of worship. Some people choose to worship God and, as a result, reap the joy that He intends for His children. Others distance themselves from God by worshiping such things as earthly possessions or personal gratification. . . . and when they do so, they suffer.

In the book of Exodus, God warns that we should place no gods before Him. Yet all too often, we place our Lord in second, third, or fourth place as we worship the gods of pride, greed, power, or lust.

When we place our desires for material possessions above our love for God—or when we yield to temptations of the flesh—we find ourselves engaged in a struggle that is similar to the one Jesus faced when He was tempted by Satan. In the wilderness, Satan offered Jesus earthly power and unimaginable riches, but Jesus turned Satan away and chose instead to worship God. We must do likewise by putting God first and worshiping only Him.

Does God rule your heart? Make certain that the honest answer to this question is a resounding yes. In the life of every righteous believer, God comes first. And that's precisely the place that He deserves in your heart, too.

MORE GREAT IDEAS ABOUT PUTTING GOD FIRST

Make God's will the focus of your life day by day. If you seek to please Him and Him alone, you'll find yourself satisfied with life.

Kay Arthur

It is impossible to please God doing things motivated by and produced by the flesh.

Bill Bright

Jesus Christ is the first and last, author and finisher, beginning and end, alpha and omega, and by Him all other things hold together. He must be first or nothing. God never comes next!

Vance Havner

You must never sacrifice
your relationship with God
for the sake of a relationship
with another person.

—

Charles Stanley

MORE FROM GOD'S WORD

Be careful not to forget the Lord.

Deuteronomy 6:12 HCSB

It is good to give thanks to the Lord, and to sing praises to Your name, O Most High; to declare Your lovingkindness in the morning, and Your faithfulness every night.

Psalm 92:1-2 NKJV

Love the Lord your God with all your heart, with all your soul, and with all your strength.

Deuteronomy 6:5 HCSB

The Devil said to Him, "I will give You their splendor and all this authority, because it has been given over to me, and I can give it to anyone I want. If You, then, will worship me, all will be Yours." And Jesus answered him, "It is written: You shall worship the Lord your God, and Him alone you shall serve."

Luke 4:6-8 HCSB

A TIP

As you establish priorities for your day and your life, God deserves first place. And you deserve the experience of putting Him there.

Write About It:
In the space below, write down your thoughts about Exodus 20:3.

ACCEPTING GOD'S ABUNDANCE

VERSE 15

*I am come that they might have life,
and that they might have it more abundantly.*

—

John 10:10 KJV

The 10th chapter of John tells us that Christ came to earth so that our lives might be filled with abundance. But what, exactly, did Jesus mean when He promised "life . . . more abundantly"? Was He referring to material possessions or financial wealth? Hardly. Jesus offers a different kind of abundance: a spiritual richness that extends beyond the temporal boundaries of this world.

Is material abundance part of God's plan for our lives? Perhaps. But in every circumstance of life, during times of wealth or times of want, God will provide us what we need if we trust Him (Matthew 6). May we, as believers, claim the riches of Christ Jesus every day that we live, and may we share His blessings with all who cross our path.

MORE GREAT IDEAS ABOUT ABUNDANCE

God loves you and wants you to experience peace and life—abundant and eternal.

Billy Graham

The gift of God is eternal life, spiritual life, abundant life through faith in Jesus Christ, the Living Word of God.

Anne Graham Lotz

God's riches are beyond anything we could ask or even dare to imagine! If my life gets gooey and stale, I have no excuse.

Barbara Johnson

Yes, we were created for His holy pleasure, but we will ultimately—if not immediately—find much pleasure in His pleasure.

Beth Moore

The only way you can experience abundant life is to surrender your plans to Him.

Charles Stanley

Jesus wants Life for us, Life with a capital L.

John Eldredge

It would be wrong to have a "poverty complex," for to think ourselves paupers is to deny either the King's riches or to deny our being His children.

Catherine Marshall

Jesus intended for us to be overwhelmed by the blessings of regular days. He said it was the reason he had come: "I am come that they might have life, and that they might have it more abundantly."

Gloria Gaither

The Bible says that being a Christian is not only a great way to die, but it's also the best way to live.

Bill Hybels

People, places, and things were never meant to give us life. God alone is the author of a fulfilling life.

Gary Smalley & John Trent

MORE FROM GOD'S WORD

Until now you have asked for nothing in My name. Ask and you will receive, that your joy may be complete.

John 16:24 HCSB

And God is able to make every grace overflow to you, so that in every way, always having everything you need, you may excel in every good work.

2 Corinthians 9:8 HCSB

My cup runs over. Surely goodness and mercy shall follow me all the days of my life; and I will dwell in the house of the Lord forever.

Psalm 23:5-6 NKJV

And He said to them, "Take heed and beware of covetousness, for one's life does not consist in the abundance of the things he possesses."

Luke 12:15 NKJV

A TIP

God wants to shower you with abundance—your job is to let Him.

WRITE ABOUT IT:
In the space below, write down your thoughts about John 10:10.

_____

_____

_____

_____

_____

_____

_____

_____

_____

_____

_____

_____

_____

_____

_____

_____

A FAMILY THAT SERVES GOD

VERSE 16

*Choose for yourselves today
the one you will worship . . . .
As for me and my family,
we will worship the Lord.*

—

Joshua 24:15 HCSB

In a world filled with countless obligations and frequent frustrations, we may be tempted to take our families for granted. But God intends otherwise.

Our families are precious gifts from our Father in heaven. If we are to be the righteous men and women that God intends, we must care for our loved ones by making time for them, even when the demands of the day are great.

Undeniably, these are difficult days for Christian households: never have distractions and temptations been greater. But, thankfully, God is bigger than all our challenges.

No family is perfect, and neither is yours. But, despite the inevitable challenges, obligations, and hurt feelings of family life, your clan is God's blessing to you. That little band of men, women, kids, and babies is a priceless treasure on temporary loan from the Father above. Give thanks to the Giver for the gift of family . . . and act accordingly.

MORE GREAT IDEAS ABOUT FAMILY

More than any other single factor in a person's formative years, family life forges character.

John Maxwell

A home is a place where we find direction.

Gigi Graham Tchividjian

One way or the other, God, who thought up the family in the first place, has the very best idea of how to bring sense to the chaos of broken relationships we see all around us. I really believe that if I remain still and listen a lot, He will share some solutions with me so I can share them with others.

Jill Briscoe

Living life with a consistent spiritual walk deeply influences those we love most.

Vonette Bright

Every Christian family ought to be, as it were, a little church, consecrated to Christ, and wholly influenced and governed by His rules.

Jonathan Edwards

Live in the present and make the most of your opportunities to enjoy your family and friends.

Barbara Johnson

A family is a place where principles are hammered and honed on the anvil of everyday living.

Charles Swindoll

Calm and peaceful, the home should be the one place where people are certain they will be welcomed, received, protected, and loved.

Ed Young

The only true source of meaning in life is found in love for God and his son Jesus Christ, and love for mankind, beginning with our own families.

James Dobson

The family that prays together, stays together.

Anonymous

MORE FROM GOD'S WORD

Now if anyone does not provide for his own relatives, and especially for his household, he has denied the faith and is worse than an unbeliever.

1 Timothy 5:8 HCSB

Love must be without hypocrisy. Detest evil; cling to what is good. Show family affection to one another with brotherly love. Outdo one another in showing honor.

Romans 12:9–10 HCSB

If a kingdom is divided against itself, that kingdom cannot stand. If a house is divided against itself, that house cannot stand.

Mark 3:24-25 HCSB

Let them first learn to show piety at home and to repay their parents; for this is good and acceptable before God.

1 Timothy 5:4 NKJV

A TIP

Your family is a precious gift from above, a gift that should be treasured, nurtured, and loved.

WRITE ABOUT IT:
In the space below, write down your thoughts about Joshua 24:15.

THE GIFT OF GRACE

VERSE 17

*For by grace you are saved through faith,
and this is not from yourselves;
it is God's gift—not from works,
so that no one can boast.*

—

Ephesians 2:8-9 HCSB

In the second chapter of Ephesians, God promises that we will be saved by faith, not by works. It's no wonder, then, that someone once said that GRACE stands for God's Redemption At Christ's Expense. It's true—God sent His Son so that we might be redeemed from our sins. In doing so, our Heavenly Father demonstrated His infinite mercy and His infinite love. We have received countless gifts from God, but none can compare with the gift of salvation. God's grace is the ultimate gift, and we owe Him the ultimate in thanksgiving.

The gift of eternal life is the priceless possession of everyone who accepts God's Son as Lord and Savior. We return our Savior's love by welcoming Him into our hearts and sharing His message and His love. When we do so, we are blessed not today and forever.

MORE GREAT IDEAS ABOUT GRACE

No one is beyond his grace. No situation, anywhere on earth, is too hard for God.

Jim Cymbala

The Christian life is motivated, not by a list of do's and don'ts, but by the gracious outpouring of God's love and blessing.

Anne Graham Lotz

In the depths of our sin, Christ died for us. He did not wait for persons to get as close as possible through obedience to the law and righteous living.

Beth Moore

God's grand strategy, birthed in his grace toward us in Christ, and nurtured through the obedience of disciplined faith, is to release us into the redeemed life of our heart, knowing it will lead us back to him even as the North Star guides a ship across the vast unknown surface of the ocean.

John Eldredge

God shields us from most of the things we fear, but when He chooses not to shield us, He unfailingly allots grace in the measure needed.

Elisabeth Elliot

How beautiful it is to learn
that grace isn't fragile,
and that in the family of God
we can fail and not be a failure.

—

Gloria Gaither

MORE FROM GOD'S WORD

For the law was given through Moses; grace and truth came through Jesus Christ.

John 1:17 HCSB

Therefore let us approach the throne of grace with boldness, so that we may receive mercy and find grace to help us at the proper time.

Hebrews 4:16 HCSB

Therefore, since we are receiving a kingdom that cannot be shaken, let us hold on to grace. By it, we may serve God acceptably, with reverence and awe.

Hebrews 12:28 HCSB

For the grace of God has appeared, with salvation for all people, instructing us to deny godlessness and worldly lusts and to live in a sensible, righteous, and godly way in the present age.

Titus 2:11-12 HCSB

A TIP

Remember that His grace is enough . . . God promises that His grace is sufficient for your needs. Believe Him.

WRITE ABOUT IT:
In the space below, write down your thoughts about God's gift of grace.

THE FUTILITY OF ANGER

VERSE 18

*Everyone must be quick to hear,
slow to speak, and slow to anger,
for man's anger does not accomplish
God's righteousness.*

—

James 1:19-20 HCSB

If you're like most people, you know a thing or two (or three) about anger. After all, everybody gets mad occasionally, and you're probably no exception.

Anger is a natural human emotion that is sometimes necessary and appropriate. Even Jesus became angry when confronted with the moneychangers in the temple (Matthew 21). Righteous indignation is an appropriate response to evil, but God does not intend that anger should rule our lives. Far from it.

Temper tantrums are usually unproductive, unattractive, unforgettable, and unnecessary. Perhaps that's why Proverbs 16:32 states that, "Controlling your temper is better than capturing a city" (NCV).

If you've allowed anger to become a regular visitor at your house, you should pray for wisdom, for patience, and for a heart that is so filled with forgiveness that it contains no room for bitterness. God will help you terminate your tantrums if you ask Him—and that's a good thing because anger and peace cannot coexist in the same mind.

If you permit yourself to throw too many tantrums, you will forfeit—at least for now—the peace that might otherwise be yours through Christ. So obey God's Word by turning away from anger today and every day. You'll be glad you did, and so will your family and friends.

MORE GREAT IDEAS ABOUT ANGER

Anger is the noise of the soul; the unseen irritant of the heart; the relentless invader of silence.

Max Lucado

Anger unresolved will only bring you woe.

Kay Arthur

Life is too short to spend it being angry, bored, or dull.

Barbara Johnson

When you get hot under the collar, make sure your heart is prayer-conditioned.

Anonymous

When you strike out in anger, you may miss the other person, but you will always hit yourself.

Jim Gallery

When something robs you of your peace of mind, ask yourself if it is worth the energy you are expending on it. If not, then put it out of your mind in an act of discipline. Every time the thought of "it" returns, refuse it.

Kay Arthur

Get rid of the poison
of built-up anger
and the acid
of long-term resentment.

—

Charles Swindoll

MORE FROM GOD'S WORD

All bitterness, anger and wrath, insult and slander must be removed from you, along with all wickedness. And be kind and compassionate to one another, forgiving one another, just as God also forgave you in Christ.

Ephesians 4:31-32 HCSB

Don't let your spirit rush to be angry, for anger abides in the heart of fools.

Ecclesiastes 7:9 HCSB

A fool's displeasure is known at once, but whoever ignores an insult is sensible.

Proverbs 12:16 HCSB

But now you must also put away all the following: anger, wrath, malice, slander, and filthy language from your mouth.

Colossians 3:8 HCSB

A TIP

Angry words are dangerous to your emotional and spiritual health, not to mention your relationships. So treat anger as an uninvited guest, and usher it away as quickly—and as quietly—as possible.

WRITE ABOUT IT:
In the space below, write down your thoughts
about the negative consequences of anger.

_____

_____

_____

_____

_____

_____

_____

_____

_____

_____

_____

_____

_____

_____

_____

_____

_____

_____

THE GOLDEN RULE

VERSE 19

Therefore, whatever you want others to do for you,
do also the same for them—
this is the Law and the Prophets.

—

Matthew 7:12 HCSB

The words of Matthew 7:12 remind us that, as believers in Christ, we are commanded to treat others as we wish to be treated. This commandment is, indeed, the Golden Rule for Christians of every generation. When we weave the thread of kindness into the very fabric of our lives, we give glory to the One who gave His life for ours.

Because we are imperfect human beings, we are, on occasion, selfish, thoughtless, or cruel. But God commands us to behave otherwise. He teaches us to rise above our own imperfections and to treat others with unselfishness and love. When we observe God's Golden Rule, we help build His kingdom here on earth. And, when we share the love of Christ, we share a priceless gift; may we share it today and every day that we live.

MORE GREAT IDEAS ABOUT THE GOLDEN RULE

The golden rule to follow to obtain spiritual understanding is not one of intellectual pursuit, but one of obedience.

Oswald Chambers

It is one of the most beautiful compensations of life that no one can sincerely try to help another without helping herself.

Barbara Johnson

The Golden Rule starts at home, but it should never stop there.

Marie T. Freeman

Choices can change our lives profoundly. The choice to mend a broken relationship, to say "yes" to a difficult assignment, to lay aside some important work to play with a child, to visit some forgotten person—these small choices may affect many lives eternally.

Gloria Gaither

Your light is the truth of the Gospel message itself as well as your witness as to Who Jesus is and what He has done for you. Don't hide it.

Anne Graham Lotz

In your desire to share the gospel, you may be the only Jesus someone else will ever meet. Be real and be involved with people.

Barbara Johnson

Love is not grabbing, or self-centered, or selfish. Real love is being able to contribute to the happiness of another person without expecting to get anything in return.

James Dobson

When you extend hospitality to others, you're not trying to impress people, you're trying to reflect God to them.

Max Lucado

Be so preoccupied with good will that you haven't room for ill will.

E. Stanley Jones

The #1 rule of friendship is the Golden one.

Criswell Freeman

MORE FROM GOD'S WORD

So we must not get tired of doing good, for we will reap at the proper time if we don't give up.

Galatians 6:9 HCSB

See that no one renders evil for evil to anyone, but always pursue what is good both for yourselves and for all.

1 Thessalonians 5:15 NKJV

If you really carry out the royal law prescribed in Scripture, You shall love your neighbor as yourself, you are doing well.

James 2:8 HCSB

Finally, all of you be of one mind, having compassion for one another; love as brothers, be tenderhearted, be courteous.

1 Peter 3:8 NKJV

And be kind and compassionate to one another, forgiving one another, just as God also forgave you in Christ.

Ephesians 4:32 HCSB

A TIP

When in doubt, be a little kinder than necessary.

WRITE ABOUT IT:
In the space below, write down your thoughts about the Golden Rule.

_____

_____

_____

_____

_____

_____

_____

_____

_____

_____

_____

_____

_____

_____

_____

_____

_____

WHERE TO PLACE
YOUR BURDENS

VERSE 20

Cast thy burden upon the LORD,
and he shall sustain thee:
he shall never suffer the righteous to be moved.

—

Psalm 55:22 KJV

God's Word contains promises upon which we, as Christians, can and must depend. The Bible is a priceless gift, a tool that God intends for us to use in every aspect of our lives. Too many Christians, however, keep their spiritual tool kits tightly closed and out of sight.

Psalm 55:22 instructs us to cast our burdens upon the Lord. And that's perfect advice for men, women, and children alike.

Are you tired? Discouraged? Fearful? Be comforted and trust the promises that God has made to you. Are you worried or anxious? Be confident in God's power. He will never desert you. Do you see a difficult future ahead? Be courageous and call upon God. He will protect you and then use you according to His purposes. Are you confused? Listen to the quiet voice of your Heavenly Father. He is not a God of confusion. Talk with Him; listen to Him; trust Him, and trust His promises. He is steadfast, and He is your Protector . . . forever.

MORE GREAT IDEAS ABOUT GOD'S SUPPORT

Faith is not merely you holding on to God—it is God holding on to you.

E. Stanley Jones

God uses our most stumbling, faltering faith-steps as the open door to His doing for us "more than we ask or think."

Catherine Marshall

God wants to reveal Himself as your heavenly Father. When you are hurting, you can run to Him and crawl up into His lap. When you wonder which way to turn, you can grasp His strong hand, and He'll guide you along life's path. When everything around you is falling apart, you'll feel your Father's arm around your shoulder to hold you together.

Lisa Whelchel

He stands fast as your rock, steadfast as your safeguard, sleepless as your watcher, valiant as your champion.

C. H. Spurgeon

Measure the size of the obstacles
against the size of God.

—

Beth Moore

MORE FROM GOD'S WORD

Peace, peace to you, and peace to your helpers! For your God helps you.

1 Chronicles 12:18 NKJV

He gives power to the weak, and to those who have no might He increases strength.

Isaiah 40:29 NKJV

Therefore whoever hears these sayings of Mine, and does them, I will liken him to a wise man who built his house on the rock: and the rain descended, the floods came, and the winds blew and beat on that house; and it did not fall, for it was founded on the rock.

Matthew 7:24-25 NKJV

I am able to do all things through Him who strengthens me.

Philippians 4:13 HCSB

A TIP

God can handle it. Corrie ten Boom advised, "God's all-sufficiency is a major. Your inability is a minor. Major in majors, not in minors." Enough said.

WRITE ABOUT IT:
In the space below, write down your thoughts about Psalm 55:22.

VERSE 21

You will show me the path of life;
in Your presence is fullness of joy;
at Your right hand are pleasures forevermore.

—

Psalm 16:11 NKJV

Life is best lived on purpose. And purpose, like everything else in the universe, begins in the heart of God. Whether you realize it or not, God has a direction for your life, a divine calling, a path along which He intends to lead you. When you welcome God into your heart and establish a genuine relationship with Him, He will begin—and He will continue—to make His purposes known.

Each morning, as the sun rises in the east, you welcome a new day, one that is filled to the brim with opportunities, with possibilities, and with God. As you contemplate God's blessings in your own life, you should prayerfully seek His guidance for the day ahead.

Discovering God's unfolding purpose for your life is a daily journey, a journey guided by the teachings of God's Holy Word. As you reflect upon God's promises and upon the meaning that those promises hold for you, ask God to lead you throughout the coming day. Let your Heavenly Father direct your steps; concentrate on what God wants you to do now, and leave the distant future in hands that are far more capable than your own: His hands.

Sometimes, God's intentions will be clear to you; other times, God's plan will seem uncertain at best. But even on those difficult days when you are unsure which way to turn, you must never lose sight of these overriding facts: God created you for a reason; He has important work for you to do; and He's waiting patiently for you to do it.

MORE GREAT IDEAS ABOUT LIVING ON PURPOSE

Continually restate to yourself what the purpose of your life is.

Oswald Chambers

His life is our light—our purpose and meaning and reason for living.

Anne Graham Lotz

The worst thing that laziness does is rob a man of spiritual purpose.

Billy Graham

In the very place where God has put us, whatever its limitations, whatever kind of work it may be, we may indeed serve the Lord Christ.

Elisabeth Elliot

How much of our lives are, well, so daily. How often our hours are filled with the mundane, seemingly unimportant things that have to be done, whether at home or work. These very "daily" tasks could become a celebration of praise. "It is through consecration," someone has said, "that drudgery is made divine."

Gigi Graham Tchividjian

Yesterday is just experience
but tomorrow is glistening
with purpose—
and today is the channel
leading from one to the other.

—

Barbara Johnson

MORE FROM GOD'S WORD

Whatever you do, do all to the glory of God.

1 Corinthians 10:31 NKJV

For it is God who is working among you both the willing and the working for His good purpose.

Philippians 2:13 HCSB

We know that all things work together for the good of those who love God: those who are called according to His purpose.

Romans 8:28 HCSB

I will instruct you and show you the way to go; with My eye on you, I will give counsel.

Psalm 32:8 HCSB

You're sons of Light, daughters of Day. We live under wide open skies and know where we stand. So let's not sleepwalk through life . . .

1 Thessalonians 5:5-6 MSG

A TIP

God has a plan for your life, a definite purpose that you can fulfill . . . or not. Your challenge is to pray for God's guidance and to follow wherever He leads.

Write About It:
In the space below, write down your thoughts about Psalm 16:11.

_____

_____

_____

_____

_____

_____

_____

_____

_____

_____

_____

_____

_____

_____

_____

_____

_____

_____

OBEDIENCE NOW

VERSE 22

Now by this we know that we know Him,
if we keep His commandments.

—

1 John 2:3 NKJV

Obedience to God is determined not by words, but by deeds. Talking about righteousness is easy; living righteously is far more difficult, especially in today's temptation-filled world.

Since God created Adam and Eve, we human beings have been rebelling against our Creator. Why? Because we are unwilling to trust God's Word, and we are unwilling to follow His commandments. God has given us a guidebook for righteous living called the Holy Bible. It contains thorough instructions which, if followed, lead to fulfillment, abundance, and salvation. But, if we choose to ignore God's commandments, the results are as predictable as they are tragic.

When we seek righteousness in our own lives—and when we seek the companionship of those who do likewise—we reap the spiritual rewards that God intends for our lives. When we behave ourselves as godly men and women, we honor God. When we live righteously and according to God's commandments, He blesses us in ways that we cannot fully understand.

Do you seek God's peace and His blessings? Then obey Him. When you're faced with a difficult choice or a powerful temptation, seek God's counsel and trust the counsel He gives. Invite God into your heart and live according to His commandments. When you do, you will be blessed today, and tomorrow, and forever.

MORE GREAT IDEAS ABOUT OBEDIENCE

Believe and do what God says. The life-changing consequences will be limitless, and the results will be confidence and peace of mind.

Franklin Graham

The cross that Jesus commands you and me to carry is the cross of submissive obedience to the will of God, even when His will includes suffering and hardship and things we don't want to do.

Anne Graham Lotz

You may not always see immediate results, but all God wants is your obedience and faithfulness.

Vonette Bright

I don't always like His decisions, but when I choose to obey Him, the act of obedience still "counts" with Him even if I'm not thrilled about it.

Beth Moore

Obedience is the outward expression of your love of God.

Henry Blackaby

Jesus is Victor. Calvary is the place of victory. Obedience is the pathway of victory. Bible study and prayer is the preparation for victory.

Corrie ten Boom

Let us never suppose that obedience is impossible or that holiness is meant only for a select few. Our Shepherd leads us in paths of righteousness—not for our name's sake but for His.

Elisabeth Elliot

God's love for His children in unconditional, no strings attached. But, God's blessings on our lives do come with a condition—obedience. If we are to receive the fullness of God's blessings, we must obey Him and keep His commandments.

Jim Gallery

We cannot rely on God's promises without obeying his commandments.

John Calvin

God uses ordinary people who are obedient to Him to do extraordinary things.

John Maxwell

MORE FROM GOD'S WORD

Who is wise and understanding among you? He should show his works by good conduct with wisdom's gentleness.

James 3:13 HCSB

I have sought You with all my heart; don't let me wander from Your commands.

Psalm 119:10 HCSB

Therefore, everyone who hears these words of Mine and acts on them will be like a sensible man who built his house on the rock. The rain fell, the rivers rose, and the winds blew and pounded that house. Yet it didn't collapse, because its foundation was on the rock.

Matthew 7:24–25 HCSB

Jesus answered, "If anyone loves Me, he will keep My word. My Father will love him, and We will come to him and make Our home with him."

John 14:23 HCSB

A TIP

Because God is just, He rewards good behavior just as surely as He punishes sin. Obedience earns God's pleasure; disobedience doesn't.

WRITE ABOUT IT:
In the space below, write down your thoughts about what it means to be obedient.

THE USE OF SCRIPTURE

VERSE 23

*All Scripture is given by inspiration of God,
and is profitable for doctrine, for reproof,
for correction, for instruction in righteousness,
that the man of God may be complete,
thoroughly equipped for every good work.*

—

2 Timothy 3:16-17 NKJV

I s Bible study a high priority for you? The answer to this simple question will determine, to a surprising extent, the quality of your life and the direction of your faith.

As you establish priorities for life, you must decide whether God's Word will be a bright spotlight that guides your path every day or a tiny nightlight that occasionally flickers in the dark. The decision to study the Bible—or not—is yours and yours alone. But make no mistake: how you choose to use your Bible will have a profound impact on you and your loved ones.

George Mueller observed, "The vigor of our spiritual lives will be in exact proportion to the place held by the Bible in our lives and in our thoughts." Think of it like this: the more you use your Bible, the more God will use you.

Perhaps you're one of those Christians who owns a bookshelf full of unread Bibles. If so, remember the old saying, "A Bible in the hand is worth two in the bookcase." Or perhaps you're one of those folks who is simply "too busy" to find time for a daily dose of prayer and Bible study. If so, remember the old adage, "It's hard to stumble when you're on your knees."

God's Word can be a roadmap to a place of righteousness and abundance. Make it your roadmap. God's wisdom can be a light to guide your steps. Claim it as your light today, tomorrow, and every day of your life—and then walk confidently in the footsteps of God's only begotten Son.

MORE GREAT IDEAS ABOUT GOD'S WORD

Help me, Lord, to be a student of Your Word, that I might be a better servant in Your world.

Jim Gallery

The Holy Spirit is the Spirit of Truth, which means He always works according to and through the Word of God whether you feel Him or not.

Anne Graham Lotz

The Bible is God's Word to man.

Kay Arthur

Either God's Word keeps you from sin, or sin keeps you from God's Word.

Corrie ten Boom

My meditation and study have shown me that, like God, His Word is holy, everlasting, absolutely true, powerful, personally fair, and never changing.

Bill Bright

The Scriptures were not given for our information, but for our transformation.

D. L. Moody

God's Word is a light not only to our path but also to our thinking. Place it in your heart today, and you will never walk in darkness.

Joni Eareckson Tada

Walking in faith brings you to the Word of God. There you will be healed, cleansed, fed, nurtured, equipped, and matured.

Kay Arthur

It takes calm, thoughtful, prayerful meditation on the Word to extract its deepest nourishment.

Vance Havner

God's voice isn't all that difficult to hear. He sometimes shouts through our pain, whispers to us while we're relaxing on vacation, occasionally, He sings to us in a song, and warns us through the sixty-six books of His written Word. It's right there, ink on paper. Count on it—that book will never lead you astray.

Charles Swindoll

MORE FROM GOD'S WORD

For the word of God is living and effective and sharper than any two-edged sword, penetrating as far as to divide soul, spirit, joints, and marrow; it is a judge of the ideas and thoughts of the heart.

Hebrews 4:12 HCSB

Heaven and earth will pass away, but My words will never pass away.

Matthew 24:35 HCSB

But the word of the Lord endures forever. And this is the word that was preached as the gospel to you.

1 Peter 1:25 HCSB

A TIP

God intends for you to use His Word as your guidebook for life . . . your intentions should be the same.

WRITE ABOUT IT:
In the space below, write down your thoughts about the importance of Bible study.

_____

_____

_____

_____

_____

_____

_____

_____

_____

_____

_____

_____

_____

_____

_____

_____

TRUST GOD'S TIMING

VERSE 24

To everything there is a season,
a time for every purpose under heaven.

—

Ecclesiastes 3:1 NKJV

Sometimes, the hardest thing to do is to wait. This is especially true when we're in a hurry and when we want things to happen now, if not sooner! But God's plan does not always happen in the way that we would like or at the time of our own choosing. Our task—as thoughtful men and women who trust in a benevolent, all-knowing Father—is to wait patiently for God to reveal Himself.

We humans know precisely what we want, and we know exactly when we want it. But, God has a far better plan for each of us. He has created a world that unfolds according to His own timetable, not ours . . . thank goodness! And if we're wise, we trust Him and we wait patiently for Him. After all, He is trustworthy, and He always knows best.

MORE GREAT IDEAS ABOUT GOD'S TIMING

God does not promise to keep us out of the storms and floods, but He does promise to sustain us in the storm, and then bring us out in due time for His glory when the storm has done its work.

Warren Wiersbe

When our plans are interrupted, his are not. His plans are proceeding exactly as scheduled, moving us always—including those minutes or hours or years which seem most useless or wasted or unendurable—toward the goal of true maturity.

Elisabeth Elliot

Your times are in His hands. He's in charge of the timetable, so wait patiently.

Kay Arthur

God's delays and His ways can be confusing because the process God uses to accomplish His will can go against human logic and common sense.

Anne Graham Lotz

Have patience. There is no time that is not God's time.

Criswell Freeman

Grass that is here today and gone tomorrow does not require much time to mature. A big oak tree that lasts for generations requires much more time to grow and mature. God is concerned about your life through eternity. Allow Him to take all the time He needs to shape you for His purposes. Larger assignments will require longer periods of preparation.

Henry Blackaby

When we read of the great Biblical leaders, we see that it was not uncommon for God to ask them to wait, not just a day or two, but for years, until God was ready for them to act.

Gloria Gaither

He wants us to have a faith that does not complain while waiting, but rejoices because we know our times are in His hands—nail-scarred hands that labor for our highest good.

Kay Arthur

The stops of a good man are ordered by the Lord as well as his steps.

George Mueller

MORE FROM GOD'S WORD

Therefore the Lord is waiting to show you mercy, and is rising up to show you compassion, for the Lord is a just God. Happy are all who wait patiently for Him.

Isaiah 30:18 HCSB

Wait for the Lord; be courageous and let your heart be strong. Wait for the Lord.

Psalm 27:14 HCSB

For My thoughts are not your thoughts, and your ways are not My ways. For as heaven is higher than earth, so My ways are higher than your ways, and My thoughts than your thoughts.

Isaiah 55:8-9 HCSB

Can you understand the secrets of God? His limits are higher than the heavens; you cannot reach them! They are deeper than the grave; you cannot understand them! His limits are longer than the earth and wider than the sea.

Job 11:7-9 NCV

A TIP

You don't know precisely what you need—or when you need it—but God does. So trust His timing.

WRITE ABOUT IT:
In the space below, write down your thoughts about Ecclesiastes 3:1.

_____

_____

_____

_____

_____

_____

_____

_____

_____

_____

_____

_____

_____

_____

_____

_____

VERSE 25

Guard your heart above all else,
for it is the source of life.

—

Proverbs 4:23 HCSB

You are near and dear to God. He loves you more than you can imagine, and He wants the very best for you. And one more thing: God wants you to guard your heart.

Every day, you are faced with choices . . . more choices than you can count. You can do the right thing, or not. You can be prudent, or not. You can be kind, and generous, and obedient to God. Or not.

Today, the world will offer you countless opportunities to let down your guard and, by doing so, make needless mistakes that may injure you or your loved ones. So be watchful and obedient. Guard your heart by giving it to your Heavenly Father; it is safe with Him.

MORE GREAT IDEAS ABOUT GUARDING YOUR HEART

The more wisdom enters our hearts, the more we will be able to trust our hearts in difficult situations.

John Eldredge

We can't stop the Adversary from whispering in our ears, but we can refuse to listen, and we can definitely refuse to respond.

Liz Curtis Higgs

Our actions are seen by people, but our motives are monitored by God.

Franklin Graham

A man's poverty before God is judged by the disposition of his heart, not by his coffers.

St. Augustine

The God who dwells in heaven is willing to dwell also in the heart of the humble believer.

Warren Wiersbe

To lose heart is to lose everything.

—

John Eldredge

MORE FROM GOD'S WORD

The peace of God, which surpasses all understanding, will guard your hearts and minds through Christ Jesus.

Philippians 4:7 NKJV

Keep your heart with all diligence, For out of it spring the issues of life. Put away from you a deceitful mouth, And put perverse lips far from you. Let your eyes look straight ahead, And your eyelids look right before you. Ponder the path of your feet, And let all your ways be established. Do not turn to the right or the left; Remove your foot from evil.

Proverbs 4:23-27 NKJV

Sow righteousness for yourselves and reap faithful love; break up your untilled ground. It is time to seek the Lord until He comes and sends righteousness on you like the rain.

Hosea 10:12 HCSB

A TIP

Today, think about the value of living a life that is pleasing to God. And while you're at it, think about the rewards that are likely to be yours when you do the right thing day in and day out.

WRITE ABOUT IT:
In the space below, write down your thoughts
about Proverbs 4:23.

_____

_____

_____

_____

_____

_____

_____

_____

_____

_____

_____

_____

_____

_____

_____

_____

_____

_____

VERSE 26

Then He said to them all,
"If anyone desires to come after Me,
let him deny himself,
and take up his cross daily,
and follow Me.
For whoever desires to save his life will lose it,
but whoever loses his life for My sake will save it."

—

Luke 9:23-24 NKJV

Jesus walks with you. Are you walking with Him? Hopefully, you will choose to walk with Him today and every day of your life.

Jesus loved you so much that He endured unspeakable humiliation and suffering for you. How will you respond to Christ's sacrifice? Will you follow the instructions of Luke 9:23 by taking up His cross and following Him? Or will you choose another path? When you place your hopes squarely at the foot of the cross, when you place Jesus squarely at the center of your life, you will be blessed. If you seek to be a worthy disciple of Jesus, you must acknowledge that He never comes "next." He is always first.

Do you hope to fulfill God's purpose for your life? Do you seek a life of abundance and peace? Do you intend to be Christian not just in name, but in deed? Then follow Christ. Follow Him by picking up His cross today and every day that you live. When you do, you will quickly discover that Christ's love has the power to change everything, including you.

MORE GREAT IDEAS ABOUT FOLLOWING JESUS

We have in Jesus Christ a perfect example of how to put God's truth into practice.

Bill Bright

As we live moment by moment under the control of the Spirit, His character, which is the character of Jesus, becomes evident to those around us.

Anne Graham Lotz

Peter said, "No, Lord!" But he had to learn that one cannot say "No" while saying "Lord" and that one cannot say "Lord" while saying "No."

Corrie ten Boom

Think of this—we may live together with Him here and now, a daily walking with Him who loved us and gave Himself for us.

Elisabeth Elliot

A disciple is a follower of Christ. That means you take on His priorities as your own. His agenda becomes your agenda. His mission becomes your mission.

Charles Stanley

Will you, with a glad and eager surrender, hand yourself and all that concerns you over into his hands? If you will do this, your soul will begin to know something of the joy of union with Christ.

Hannah Whitall Smith

The Christian faith is meant to be lived moment by moment. It isn't some broad, general outline—it's a long walk with a real Person. Details count: passing thoughts, small sacrifices, a few encouraging words, little acts of kindness, brief victories over nagging sins.

Joni Eareckson Tada

Our battles are first won or lost in the secret places of our will in God's presence, never in full view of the world.

Oswald Chambers

The essence of the Christian life is Jesus: that in all things He might have the preeminence, not that in some things He might have a place.

Franklin Graham

To walk out of His will is to walk into nowhere.

C. S. Lewis

MORE FROM GOD'S WORD

The next day John saw Jesus coming toward him and said, "Here is the Lamb of God, who takes away the sin of the world!"

John 1:29 HCSB

But whoever keeps His word, truly in him the love of God is perfected. This is how we know we are in Him: the one who says he remains in Him should walk just as He walked.

1 John 2:5-6 HCSB

We encouraged, comforted, and implored each one of you to walk worthy of God, who calls you into His own kingdom and glory.

1 Thessalonians 2:12 HCSB

"Follow Me," Jesus told them, "and I will make you into fishers of men!" Immediately they left their nets and followed Him.

Mark 1:17-18 HCSB

A TIP

It takes a radical commitment—and significant sacrifices—to really follow Jesus. And it's worth it.

Write About It:

In the space below, write down your thoughts about what it means to follow Jesus.

_____

_____

_____

_____

_____

_____

_____

_____

_____

_____

_____

_____

_____

_____

_____

_____

_____

CHRIST'S LOVE

VERSE 27

As the Father loved Me,
I also have loved you;
abide in My love.

—

John 15:9 NKJV

How much does Christ love us? More than we, as mere mortals, can comprehend. His love is perfect and steadfast. Even though we are fallible and wayward, the Good Shepherd cares for us still. Even though we have fallen far short of the Father's commandments, Christ loves us with a power and depth that are beyond our understanding. The sacrifice that Jesus made upon the cross was made for each of us, and His love endures to the edge of eternity and beyond.

Hannah Whitall Smith spoke to believers of every generation when she advised, "Keep your face upturned to Christ as the flowers do to the sun. Look, and your soul shall live and grow." How true. When we turn our hearts to Jesus, we receive His blessings, His peace, and His grace.

Christ is the ultimate Savior of mankind and the personal Savior of those who believe in Him. As His servants, we should place Him at the very center of our lives. And, every day that God gives us breath, we should share Christ's love and His message with a world that needs both.

Christ's love changes everything. When you accept His gift of grace, you are transformed, not only for today, but also for all eternity. If you haven't already done so, accept Jesus Christ as your personal Savior. He's waiting patiently for you to invite Him into your heart. Please don't make Him wait a single minute longer.

MORE GREAT IDEAS ABOUT CHRIST'S LOVE

No man ever loved like Jesus. He taught the blind to see and the dumb to speak. He died on the cross to save us. He bore our sins. And now God says, "Because He did, I can forgive you."

Billy Graham

To God be the glory, great things He has done; / So loved He the world that He gave us His Son.

Fanny Crosby

Live your lives in love, the same sort of love which Christ gives us, and which He perfectly expressed when He gave Himself as a sacrifice to God.

Corrie ten Boom

This hard place in which you perhaps find yourself is the very place in which God is giving you opportunity to look only to Him, to spend time in prayer, and to learn long-suffering, gentleness, meekness—in short, to learn the depths of the love that Christ Himself has poured out on all of us.

Elisabeth Elliot

The richest meaning of your life is contained in the idea that Christ loved you enough to give His life for you.

Calvin Miller

Jesus loves me! This I know, for the Bible tells me so. Little ones to him belong; they are weak, but he is strong. / Yes, Jesus loves me! Yes, Jesus loves me! Yes, Jesus loves me! The Bible tells me so.

Anna B. Warner and Susan Warner

Sometimes Agape really hurts. It broke the heart of God to demonstrate His love to us through Christ but its ultimate end was salvation.

Beth Moore

Christ is like a river that is continually flowing. There are always fresh supplies of water coming from the fountainhead, so that a man may live by it and be supplied with water all his life. So Christ is an ever-flowing fountain; he is continually supplying his people, and the fountain is not spent. They who live upon Christ may have fresh supplies from him for all eternity; they may have an increase of blessedness that is new, and new still, and which never will come to an end.

Jonathan Edwards

MORE FROM GOD'S WORD

Who can separate us from the love of Christ? Can affliction or anguish or persecution or famine or nakedness or danger or sword? . . . No, in all these things we are more than victorious through Him who loved us.

Romans 8:35, 37 HCSB

I am the good shepherd. The good shepherd lays down his life for the sheep.

John 10:11 HCSB

But God proves His own love for us in that while we were still sinners Christ died for us!

Romans 5:8 HCSB

No one has greater love than this, that someone would lay down his life for his friends.

John 15:13 HCSB

A TIP

Jesus loves you. His love can—and should—be the cornerstone and the touchstone of your life.

WRITE ABOUT IT:
In the space below, write down your thoughts about John 15:9.

STAYING HUMBLE

VERSE 28

The greatest among you must be a servant.
But those who exalt themselves will be humbled,
and those who humble themselves will be exalted.

—

Matthew 23:11-12 NKJV

As fallible human beings, we have so much to be humble about. Why, then, is humility such a difficult trait for us to master? Precisely because we are fallible human beings. Yet if we are to grow and mature as Christians, we must strive to give credit where credit is due, starting, of course, with God and His only begotten Son.

As Christians, we have been refashioned and saved by Jesus Christ, and that salvation came not because of our own good works but because of God's grace. Thus, we are not "self-made"; we are "God-made" and we are "Christ-saved." How, then, can we be boastful? The answer, of course, is that, if we are honest with ourselves and with our God, we simply can't be boastful . . . we must, instead, be eternally grateful and exceedingly humble. Humility, however, is not easy for most of us. All too often, we are tempted to stick out our chests and say, "Look at me; look what I did!" But, in the quiet moments when we search the depths of our own hearts, we know better. Whatever "it" is, God did that. And He deserves the credit.

MORE GREAT IDEAS ABOUT HUMILITY

I can usually sense that a leading is from the Holy Spirit when it calls me to humble myself, to serve somebody, to encourage somebody, or to give something away. Very rarely will the evil one lead us to do those kind of things.

Bill Hybels

If you know who you are in Christ, your personal ego is not an issue.

Beth Moore

That's what I love about serving God. In His eyes, there are no little people . . . because there are no big people. We are all on the same playing field. We all start at square one. No one has it better than the other, or possesses unfair advantage.

Joni Eareckson Tada

We are never stronger than the moment we admit we are weak.

Beth Moore

Faith itself cannot be strong where humility is weak.

C. H. Spurgeon

Because Christ Jesus came to the world clothed in humility, he will always be found among those who are clothed with humility. He will be found among the humble people.

A. W. Tozer

That some of my hymns have been dictated by the blessed Holy Spirit I have no doubt; and that others have been the result of deep meditation I know to be true; but that the poet has any right to claim special merit for himself is certainly presumptuous.

Fanny Crosby

All kindness and good deeds, we must keep silent. The result will be an inner reservoir of personality power.

Catherine Marshall

Jesus had a humble heart. If He abides in us, pride will never dominate our lives.

Billy Graham

Humility is the fairest and rarest flower that blooms.

Charles Swindoll

MORE FROM GOD'S WORD

Clothe yourselves with humility toward one another, because God resists the proud, but gives grace to the humble.

1 Peter 5:5 HCSB

But He said to me, "My grace is sufficient for you, for power is perfected in weakness." Therefore, I will most gladly boast all the more about my weaknesses, so that Christ's power may reside in me.

2 Corinthians 12:9 HCSB

You will save the humble people; But Your eyes are on the haughty, that You may bring them down.

2 Samuel 22:28 NKJV

If My people who are called by My name will humble themselves, and pray and seek My face, and turn from their wicked ways, then I will hear from heaven, and will forgive their sin and heal their land.

2 Chronicles 7:14 NKJV

A TIP

You must remain humble or face the consequences. Pride does go before the fall, but humility often prevents the fall.

WRITE ABOUT IT:
In the space below, write down your thoughts about Matthew 23:11-12.

VERSE 29

These things have I spoken unto you,
that my joy might remain in you,
and that your joy might be full.

—

John 15:11 KJV

Christ made it clear: He intends that His joy should become our joy. Yet sometimes, amid the inevitable hustle and bustle of life here on earth, we can forfeit—albeit temporarily—the joy of Christ as we wrestle with the challenges of daily living.

Jonathan Edwards, the 18th-century American clergyman, observed, "Christ is not only a remedy for your weariness and trouble, but he will give you an abundance of the contrary: joy and delight. They who come to Christ do not only come to a resting-place after they have been wandering in a wilderness, but they come to a banqueting-house where they may rest, and where they may feast. They may cease from their former troubles and toils, and they may enter upon a course of delights and spiritual joys."

If, today, your heart is heavy, open the door of your soul to Christ. He will give you peace and joy. And, if you already have the joy of Christ in your heart, share it freely, just as Christ freely shared His joy with you.

MORE GREAT IDEAS ABOUT JOY

Joy is the direct result of having God's perspective on our daily lives and the effect of loving our Lord enough to obey His commands and trust His promises.

Bill Bright

If you can forgive the person you were, accept the person you are, and believe in the person you will become, you are headed for joy. So celebrate your life.

Barbara Johnson

The Christian lifestyle is not one of legalistic do's and don'ts, but one that is positive, attractive, and joyful.

Vonette Bright

Lord, I thank you for the promise of heaven and the unexpected moments when you touch my heartstrings with that longing for my eternal home.

Joni Eareckson Tada

Our sense of joy, satisfaction, and fulfillment in life increases, no matter what the circumstances, if we are in the center of God's will.

Billy Graham

Joy is the heart's
harmonious response
to the Lord's song of love.

—

A. W. Tozer

MORE FROM GOD'S WORD

Rejoice, and be exceeding glad: for great is your reward in heaven . . . .

Matthew 5:12 KJV

Rejoice in the Lord always. I will say it again: Rejoice!

Philippians 4:4 HCSB

Delight yourself also in the Lord, and He shall give you the desires of your heart.

Psalm 37:4 NKJV

Make me hear joy and gladness.

Psalm 51:8 NKJV

Weeping may spend the night, but there is joy in the morning.

Psalm 30:5 HCSB

A TIP

Every day, God gives you many reasons to rejoice. The rest is up to you.

WRITE ABOUT IT:

In the space below, write down your thoughts about the need to share Christ's joy with family, with friends, and with the world.

_____

_____

_____

_____

_____

_____

_____

_____

_____

_____

_____

_____

_____

_____

_____

_____

_____

_____

REJOICE!

VERSE 30

Rejoice in the Lord always.
Again I will say, rejoice!

—

Philippians 4:4 NKJV

Are you living a life of agitation, consternation, or celebration? If you're a believer, it should most certainly be the latter. With Christ as your Savior, every day should be a time of celebration.

Oswald Chambers correctly observed, "Joy is the great note all throughout the Bible." C. S. Lewis echoed that thought when he wrote, "Joy is the serious business of heaven." But, even the most dedicated Christians can, on occasion, forget to celebrate each day for what it is: a priceless gift from God.

Today, celebrate the life that God has given you. Today, put a smile on your face, kind words on your lips, and a song in your heart. Be generous with your praise and free with your encouragement. And then, when you have celebrated life to the fullest, invite your friends to do likewise. After all, this is God's day, and He has given us clear instructions for its use. We are commanded to rejoice and be glad. So, with no further ado, let the celebration begin . . .

MORE GREAT IDEAS ABOUT CELEBRATION

Joy is the direct result of having God's perspective on our daily lives and the effect of loving our Lord enough to obey His commands and trust His promises.

Bill Bright

According to Jesus, it is God's will that His children be filled with the joy of life.

Catherine Marshall

If you can forgive the person you were, accept the person you are, and believe in the person you will become, you are headed for joy. So celebrate your life.

Barbara Johnson

Christ is the secret, the source, the substance, the center, and the circumference of all true and lasting gladness.

Mrs. Charles E. Cowman

A life of intimacy with God is characterized by joy.

Oswald Chambers

When we get rid of inner conflicts and wrong attitudes toward life, we will almost automatically burst into joy.

E. Stanley Jones

185

Our sense of joy, satisfaction, and fulfillment in life increases, no matter what the circumstances, if we are in the center of God's will.

Billy Graham

When the dream of our heart is one that God has planted there, a strange happiness flows into us. At that moment, all of the spiritual resources of the universe are released to help us. Our praying is then at one with the will of God and becomes a channel for the Creator's purposes for us and our world.

Catherine Marshall

Joy is a by-product not of happy circumstances, education or talent, but of a healthy relationship with God and a determination to love Him no matter what.

Barbara Johnson

Some of us seem so anxious about avoiding hell that we forget to celebrate our journey toward heaven.

Philip Yancey

MORE FROM GOD'S WORD

This is the day the LORD has made; we will rejoice and be glad in it.

Psalm 118:24 NKJV

If they serve Him obediently, they will end their days in prosperity and their years in happiness.

Job 36:11 HCSB

The one who understands a matter finds success, and the one who trusts in the Lord will be happy.

Proverbs 16:20 HCSB

How happy is the man who does not follow the advice of the wicked, or take the path of sinners, or join a group of mockers!

Psalm 1:1 HCSB

A TIP

Every day should be a cause for celebration. By celebrating the gift of life, you protect your heart from the dangers of pessimism, regret, hopelessness, and bitterness.

WRITE ABOUT IT:
In the space below, write down your thoughts about Philippians 4:4.

_____

_____

_____

_____

_____

_____

_____

_____

_____

_____

_____

_____

_____

_____

_____

_____

_____

_____

FORGIVENESS: YES, JUDGING: NO

VERSE 31

Do not judge, and you will not be judged.
Do not condemn, and you will not be condemned.
Forgive, and you will be forgiven.

—

Luke 6:37 HCSB

Even the most devoted Christians may fall prey to a powerful yet subtle temptation: the temptation to judge others. But as Christians, we are commanded to refrain from such behavior. The warning of Luke 6:37 is clear: "Do not judge." Yet, as fallible, imperfect human beings living in a stressful world, we are sorely tempted to do otherwise.

As Jesus came upon a young woman who had been condemned by the Pharisees, He spoke not only to the crowd that was gathered there, but also to all generations when He warned, "He that is without sin among you, let him first cast a stone at her" (John 8:7 KJV). Christ's message is clear, and it applies not only to the Pharisees of ancient times, but also to us.

We have all fallen short of God's commandments, and none of us, therefore, are qualified to "cast the first stone." Thankfully, God has forgiven us, and we, too, must forgive others. As Christian believers, we are warned that to judge others is to invite fearful consequences: to the extent we judge others, so, too, will we be judged by God. Let us refrain, then, from judging our neighbors. Instead, let us forgive them and love them in the same way that God has forgiven us.

MORE GREAT IDEAS ABOUT JUDGING OTHERS

Judging draws the judgment of others.

Catherine Marshall

Christians think they are prosecuting attorneys or judges, when, in reality, God has called all of us to be witnesses.

Warren Wiersbe

Don't judge other people more harshly than you want God to judge you.

Marie T. Freeman

An individual Christian may see fit to give up all sorts of things for special reasons—marriage, or meat, or beer, or cinema; but the moment he starts saying these things are bad in themselves, or looking down his nose at other people who do use them, he has taken the wrong turn.

C. S. Lewis

Being critical of others, including God, is one way we try to avoid facing and judging our own sins.

Warren Wiersbe

Finally, all of you be of one mind, having compassion for one another; love as brothers, be tenderhearted, be courteous.

—

1 Peter 3:8 NKJV

MORE FROM GOD'S WORD

Speak and act as those who will be judged by the law of freedom. For judgment is without mercy to the one who hasn't shown mercy. Mercy triumphs over judgment.

James 2:12-13 HCSB

When Jesus stood up, He said to her, "Woman, where are they? Has no one condemned you?" "No one, Lord," she answered. "Neither do I condemn you," said Jesus. "Go, and from now on do not sin any more."

John 8:10-11 HCSB

Therefore judge nothing before the time, until the Lord comes, who will both bring to light the hidden things of darkness and reveal the counsels of the hearts. Then each one's praise will come from God.

1 Corinthians 4:5 NKJV

A TIP

To the extent you judge others, so, too, will you be judged. So you must, to the best of your ability, refrain from judgmental thoughts and words.

WRITE ABOUT IT:
In the space below, write down your thoughts about Luke 6:37.

_____

_____

_____

_____

_____

_____

_____

_____

_____

_____

_____

_____

_____

_____

_____

_____

_____

_____

GENEROSITY NOW

VERSE 32

Assuredly, I say to you,
inasmuch as you did it to one of the least
of these My brethren, you did it to Me.

—

Matthew 25:40 NKJV

In the busyness and confusion of daily life, it is easy to lose focus, and it is easy to become frustrated. We are imperfect human beings struggling to manage our lives as best we can, but we often fall short. When we are distracted or disappointed, we may neglect to share a kind word or a kind deed. This oversight hurts others, but it hurts us most of all.

Matthew 25:40 warns, "Inasmuch as you did it to one of the least of these My brethren, you did it to Me." When we extend the hand of friendship to those who need it most, God promises His blessings. When we ignore the needs of others—or mistreat them—we risk God's retribution.

Today, slow yourself down and be alert for those who need your smile, your kind words, or your helping hand. Make kindness a centerpiece of your dealings with others. They will be blessed, and you will be, too. When you spread a heaping helping of encouragement and hope to the world, you can't help getting a little bit on yourself.

MORE GREAT IDEAS ABOUT KINDNESS

When you extend hospitality to others, you're not trying to impress people, you're trying to reflect God to them.

Max Lucado

When we do little acts of kindness that make life more bearable for someone else, we are walking in love as the Bible commands us.

Barbara Johnson

It is one of the most beautiful compensations of life that no one can sincerely try to help another without helping herself.

Barbara Johnson

The mark of a Christian is that he will walk the second mile and turn the other cheek. A wise man or woman gives the extra effort, all for the glory of the Lord Jesus Christ.

John Maxwell

Be so preoccupied with good will that you haven't room for ill will.

E. Stanley Jones

Do all the good you can. By all the means you can. In all the ways you can. In all the places you can. At all the times you can. To all the people you can. As long as ever you can.

John Wesley

When we Christians are too busy to care for each other, we're simply too busy for our own good . . . and for God's.

Marie T. Freeman

If I am inconsiderate about the comfort of others, or their feelings, or even their little weaknesses; if I am careless about their little hurts and miss opportunities to smooth their way; if I make the sweet running of household wheels more difficult to accomplish, then I know nothing of Calvary's love.

Amy Carmichael

Scientists tell us that every word and picture ever broadcast electronically is still somewhere out in space, billions of miles away. If humans ever go to other planets, they may see an old episode of "Gunsmoke." Amazing as that sounds, there is something even more astonishing: Not a single act of goodness in Jesus' name has ever disappeared. Every act of kindness reaches out and touches the lives of thousands of people—one at a time.

Dennis Swanberg

MORE FROM GOD'S WORD

Finally, all of you be of one mind, having compassion for one another; love as brothers, be tenderhearted, be courteous.

1 Peter 3:8 NKJV

A kind man benefits himself, but a cruel man brings disaster on himself.

Proverbs 11:17 HCSB

Love is patient; love is kind.

1 Corinthians 13:4 HCSB

Therefore, God's chosen ones, holy and loved, put on heartfelt compassion, kindness, humility, gentleness, and patience.

Colossians 3:12 HCSB

And be kind and compassionate to one another, forgiving one another, just as God also forgave you in Christ.

Ephesians 4:32 HCSB

A TIP

Kind words have echoes that last a lifetime and beyond.

WRITE ABOUT IT:
In the space below, write down your thoughts
about Matthew 25:40.

_____

_____

_____

_____

_____

_____

_____

_____

_____

_____

_____

_____

_____

_____

_____

_____

THE DIRECTION OF
YOUR THOUGHTS

VERSE 33

Finally, brethren, whatever things are true,
whatever things are noble,
whatever things are just,
whatever things are pure,
whatever things are lovely,
whatever things are of good report,
if there is any virtue
and if there is anything praiseworthy—
meditate on these things.

—

Philippians 4:8 NKJV

How will you direct your thoughts today? Will you obey the words of Philippians 4:8 by dwelling upon those things that are true, noble, and just? Or will you allow your thoughts to be hijacked by the negativity that seems to dominate our troubled world?

Are you fearful, angry, bored, or worried? Are you so preoccupied with the concerns of this day that you fail to thank God for the promise of eternity? Are you confused, bitter, or pessimistic? If so, God wants to have a little talk with you.

God intends that you be an ambassador for Him, an enthusiastic, hope-filled Christian. But God won't force you to adopt a positive attitude. It's up to you to think positively about your blessings and opportunities . . . or not. So, today and every day hereafter, celebrate this life that God has given you by focusing your thoughts and your energies upon "things that are excellent and worthy of praise." Today, count your blessings instead of your hardships. And thank the Giver of all things good for gifts that are simply too numerous to count.

MORE GREAT IDEAS ABOUT YOUR THOUGHTS

It is the thoughts and intents of the heart that shape a person's life.

John Eldredge

Preoccupy my thoughts with your praise beginning today.

Joni Eareckson Tada

Attitude is the mind's paintbrush; it can color any situation.

Barbara Johnson

As we have by faith said no to sin, so we should by faith say yes to God and set our minds on things above, where Christ is seated in the heavenlies.

Vonette Bright

Whether we think of, or speak to, God, whether we act or suffer for him, all is prayer when we have no other object than his love and the desire of pleasing him.

John Wesley

Every major spiritual battle is in the mind.

Charles Stanley

No more imperfect thoughts. No more sad memories. No more ignorance. My redeemed body will have a redeemed mind. Grant me a foretaste of that perfect mind as you mirror your thoughts in me today.

Joni Eareckson Tada

The things we think are the things that feed our souls. If we think on pure and lovely things, we shall grow pure and lovely like them; and the converse is equally true.

Hannah Whitall Smith

Your thoughts are the determining factor as to whose mold you are conformed to. Control your thoughts and you control the direction of your life.

Charles Stanley

Beware of cut-and-dried theologies that reduce the ways of God to a manageable formula that keeps life safe. God often does the unexplainable just to keep us on our toes—and also on our knees.

Warren Wiersbe

MORE FROM GOD'S WORD

Guard your heart above all else, for it is the source of life.

Proverbs 4:23 HCSB

Set your minds on what is above, not on what is on the earth.

Colossians 3:2 HCSB

Commit your works to the Lord, and your thoughts will be established.

Proverbs 16:3 NKJV

Brothers, don't be childish in your thinking, but be infants in evil and adult in your thinking.

1 Corinthians 14:20 HCSB

May the words of my mouth and the meditation of my heart be acceptable to You, Lord, my rock and my Redeemer.

Psalm 19:14 HCSB

A TIP

Either you can control your thoughts, or they most certainly will control you.

WRITE ABOUT IT:
In the space below, write down your thoughts
about Philippians 4:8.

_____

_____

_____

_____

_____

_____

_____

_____

_____

_____

_____

_____

_____

_____

_____

_____

_____

VERSE 34

*I have come as a light into the world,
that whoever believes in Me
should not abide in darkness.*

—

John 12:46 NKJV

The words of John 12:46 teach us that Jesus is the light of the world. And, John 14:6 instructs us that Jesus is, "the way, the truth, and the life." Without Christ, we are as far removed from salvation as the east is removed from the west. And without Christ, we can never know the ultimate truth: God's truth.

Truth is God's way: He commands His believers to live in truth, and He rewards those who do so. Jesus is the personification of God's liberating truth, a truth that offers salvation to mankind.

Do you seek to walk with God? Do you seek to feel His presence and His peace? Then you must walk in truth; you must walk in the light; you must walk with the Savior. There is simply no other way.

MORE GREAT IDEAS ABOUT JESUS

When you can't see him, trust him. Jesus is closer than you ever dreamed.

Max Lucado

I am truly happy with Jesus Christ. I couldn't live without Him. When my life gets beyond the ability to cope, He takes over.

Ruth Bell Graham

There was One, who for "us sinners and our salvation," left the glories of heaven and sojourned upon this earth in weariness and woe, amid those who hated his and finally took his life.

Lottie Moon

In your greatest weakness, turn to your greatest strength, Jesus, and hear Him say, "My grace is sufficient for you, for My strength is made perfect in weakness" (2 Corinthians 12:9, NKJV).

Lisa Whelchel

The key to my understanding of the Bible is a personal relationship to Jesus Christ.

Oswald Chambers

Christians see sin for what it is: willful rebellion against the rulership of God in their lives. And in turning from their sin, they have embraced God's only means of dealing with sin: Jesus.

Kay Arthur

When we are in a situation where Jesus is all we have, we soon discover he is all we really need.

Gigi Graham Tchividjian

Jesus: the proof of God's love.

Philip Yancey

Jesus—personally, socially, politically, the supreme center of human interest today.

R. G. Lee

Jesus Christ is the first and last, author and finisher, beginning and end, alpha and omega, and by Him all other things hold together. He must be first or nothing. God never comes next!

Vance Havner

MORE FROM GOD'S WORD

For unto us a Child is born, Unto us a Son is given; And the government will be upon His shoulder. And His name will be called Wonderful, Counselor, Mighty God, Everlasting Father, Prince of Peace.

Isaiah 9:6 NKJV

The next day John saw Jesus coming toward him and said, "Here is the Lamb of God, who takes away the sin of the world!"

John 1:29 HCSB

But we do see Jesus—made lower than the angels for a short time so that by God's grace He might taste death for everyone— crowned with glory and honor because of the suffering of death.

Hebrews 2:9 HCSB

I am the door. If anyone enters by Me, he will be saved.

John 10:9 NKJV

A TIP

You are a light upon the world around you. Make sure that your light is both bright and good.

WRITE ABOUT IT:
In the space below, write down your thoughts about John 12:46.

_____

_____

_____

_____

_____

_____

_____

_____

_____

_____

_____

_____

_____

_____

_____

_____

_____

KEEPING MONEY IN PERSPECTIVE

VERSE 35

No one can be a slave of two masters,
since either he will hate one and love the other,
or be devoted to one and despise the other.
You cannot be slaves of God and of money.

—

Matthew 6:24 HCSB

Your money can be used as a blessing to yourself and to your loved ones, but beware: You live in a society that places far too much importance on money and the things that money can buy. God does not. God cares about people, not possessions, and so must you.

Money, in and of itself, is not evil, but worshipping money most certainly is. So today, as you prioritize matters of importance for you and yours, remember that God is almighty, but the dollar is not.

When we worship God, we are blessed. But if we worship "the almighty dollar," we inevitably pay a price for our misplaced priorities—and our punishment inevitably comes sooner rather than later. Our challenge, then, is to keep money in proper perspective which, by the way, is God's perspective.

MORE GREAT IDEAS ABOUT KEEPING MONEY IN PERSPECTIVE

One of the dangers of having a lot of money is that you may be quite satisfied with the kinds of happiness money can give and so fail to realize your need for God. If everything seems to come simply by signing checks, you may forget that you are at every moment totally dependent on God.

C. S. Lewis

Have you prayed about your resources lately? Find out how God wants you to use your time and your money. No matter what it costs, forsake all that is not of God.

Kay Arthur

Your priorities, passions, goals, and fears are shown clearly in the flow of your money.

Dave Ramsey

God is entitled to a portion of our income. Not because he needs it, but because we need to give it.

James Dobson

Everything that we own belongs to God—including money—and He will use it to direct our lives.

Larry Burkett

Servants of God are always more concerned about ministry than money.

Rick Warren

Attitude is always God's concern. Christ's statement dealing with the rich young ruler was based on that man's attitude, his motivation, and the purpose behind his money.

Larry Burkett

If a person gets his attitude toward money straight, it wil help straighten out almost every other area of his life.

Billy Graham

Money is a mirror that, strange as it sounds, reflects our personal weaknesses and strengths with amazing clarity.

Dave Ramsey

TITHE! Anyone can honk!

Anonymous

MORE FROM GOD'S WORD

Your life should be free from the love of money. Be satisfied with what you have, for He Himself has said, I will never leave you or forsake you.

Hebrews 13:5 HCSB

The borrower is a slave to the lender.

Proverbs 22:7 HCSB

Based on the gift they have received, everyone should use it to serve others, as good managers of the varied grace of God.

1 Peter 4:10 HCSB

The one who loves money is never satisfied with money, and whoever loves wealth [is] never [satisfied] with income. This too is futile.

Ecclesiastes 5:10 HCSB

A TIP

The Bible warns us never to fall in love with money.

WRITE ABOUT IT:
In the space below, write down your thoughts about Matthew 6:24.

_____

_____

_____

_____

_____

_____

_____

_____

_____

_____

_____

_____

_____

_____

_____

_____

BE MERCIFUL

VERSE 36

Blessed are the merciful,
because they will be shown mercy.

—

Matthew 5:7 HCSB

If we wish to build lasting relationships, we must learn how to forgive. Why? Because our loved ones are imperfect (as are we). How often must we forgive our spouses and our friends? More times than we can count; to do otherwise is to disobey God.

Are you easily frustrated by the inevitable imperfections of others? Are you easily angered? Do you sometimes hold on to feelings of bitterness and regret. If so, perhaps you need a refresher course in the art of forgiveness.

Perhaps granting forgiveness is hard for you. If so, you are not alone. Genuine, lasting forgiveness is often difficult to achieve—difficult but not impossible. Thankfully, with God's help, all things are possible, and that includes forgiveness. But even though God is willing to help, He expects you to do some of the work.

If there exists even one person, alive or dead, whom you have not forgiven (and that includes yourself and, of course, your spouse), follow God's commandment and His will for your life: forgive. Bitterness, anger, and regret are not part of God's plan for your life. Forgiveness is.

MORE GREAT IDEAS ABOUT
LOVE AND FORGIVENESS

Jesus had a forgiving and understanding heart. If he lives within us, mercy will temper our relationships with our fellow men.

Billy Graham

The fact is, God no longer deals with us in judgment but in mercy. If people got what they deserved, this old planet would have ripped apart at the seams centuries ago. Praise God that because of His great love "we are not consumed, for his compassions never fail" (Lam. 3:22).

Joni Eareckson Tada

When God forgives, He forgets. He buries our sins in the sea and puts a sign on the shore saying, "No Fishing Allowed."

Corrie ten Boom

God expects us to forgive others as He has forgiven us; we are to follow His example by having a forgiving heart.

Vonette Bright

Revenge is the raging fire that consumes the arsonist.

Max Lucado

The more you practice the art of forgiving, the quicker you'll master the art of living.

Marie T. Freeman

Forgiveness is the precondition of love.

Catherine Marshall

To hold on to hate and resentments is to throw a monkey wrench into the machinery of life.

E. Stanley Jones

Our forgiveness toward others should flow from a realization and appreciation of God's forgiveness toward us.

Franklin Graham

By not forgiving, by not letting wrongs go, we aren't getting back at anyone. We are merely punishing ourselves by barricading our own hearts.

Jim Cymbala

MORE FROM GOD'S WORD

Be merciful, just as your Father also is merciful.

Luke 6:36 HCSB

And whenever you stand praying, if you have anything against anyone, forgive him, so that your Father in heaven may also forgive you your wrongdoing.

Mark 11:25 HCSB

For if you forgive people their wrongdoing, your heavenly Father will forgive you as well. But if you don't forgive people, your Father will not forgive your wrongdoing.

Matthew 6:14-15 HCSB

All bitterness, anger and wrath, insult and slander must be removed from you, along with all wickedness. And be kind and compassionate to one another, forgiving one another, just as God also forgave you in Christ.

Ephesians 4:31-32 HCSB

A TIP

You should love all people, including your enemies. It's a difficult job, but with God's help, you can do it.

WRITE ABOUT IT:
In the space below, write down your thoughts about Matthew 5:7.

_____

_____

_____

_____

_____

_____

_____

_____

_____

_____

_____

_____

_____

_____

_____

_____

_____

THE NEW YOU

VERSE 37

Therefore, if anyone is in Christ,
he is a new creation;
old things have passed away;
behold, all things have become new.

—

2 Corinthians 5:17 NKJV

In 2 Corinthians 5:17, we are told that when a person accepts Christ, he or she becomes a new creation. Have you invited God's Son to reign over your heart and your life? If so, think for a moment about the "old" you, the person you were before you invited Christ into your heart. Now, think about the "new" you, the person you have become since then. Is there a difference between the "old" you and the "new and improved" version? There should be! And that difference should be noticeable not only to you but also to others.

Warren Wiersbe observed, "The greatest miracle of all is the transformation of a lost sinner into a child of God." And Oswald Chambers noted, "If the Spirit of God has transformed you within, you will exhibit Divine characteristics in your life, not good human characteristics. God's life in us expresses itself as God's life, not as a human life trying to be godly."

When you invited Christ to reign over your heart, you became a new creation through Him. This day offers yet another opportunity to behave yourself like that new creation by serving your Creator and strengthening your character. When you do, God will guide your steps and bless your endeavors today and forever.

MORE GREAT IDEAS ABOUT CONVERSION

God is not a supernatural interferer; God is the everlasting portion of his people. When a man born from above begins his new life, he meets God at every turn, hears him in every sound, sleeps at his feet, and wakes to find him there.

Oswald Chambers

The amazing thing about Jesus is that He doesn't just patch up our lives, He gives us a brand new sheet, a clean slate to start over, all new.

Gloria Gaither

Be filled with the Holy Spirit; join a church where the members believe the Bible and know the Lord; seek the fellowship of other Christians; learn and be nourished by God's Word and His many promises. Conversion is not the end of your journey—it is only the beginning.

Corrie ten Boom

If we accept His invitation to salvation, we live with Him forever. However, if we do not accept because we refuse His only Son as our Savior, then we exclude ourselves from My Father's House. It's our choice.

Anne Graham Lotz

Has he taken over your heart? Perhaps he resides there, but does he preside there?

Vance Havner

If you are God's child, you are no longer bound to your past or to what you were. You are a brand new creature in Christ Jesus.

Kay Arthur

Being born again is God's solution to our need for love and life and light.

Anne Graham Lotz

Before God changes our circumstances, He wants to change our hearts.

Warren Wiersbe

No one can be converted except with the consent of his own free will because God does not override human choice.

Billy Graham

We had better quickly discover whether we have mere religion or a real experience with Jesus, whether we have outward observance of religious forms or hearts that beat in tune with God.

Jim Cymbala

MORE FROM GOD'S WORD

And we have seen and testify that the Father has sent his Son to be the Savior of the world.

1 John 4:14 NIV

Then He called a child to Him and had him stand among them. "I assure you," He said, "unless you are converted and become like children, you will never enter the kingdom of heaven."

Matthew 18:2-3 HCSB

Therefore we were buried with Him by baptism into death, in order that, just as Christ was raised from the dead by the glory of the Father, so we too may walk in a new way of life.

Romans 6:4 HCSB

Everyone who believes that Jesus is the Messiah has been born of God, and everyone who loves the parent also loves his child.

1 John 5:1 HCSB

A TIP

Unless you're a radically different person because of your relationship with Jesus, your faith isn't what it could be . . . or should be.

WRITE ABOUT IT:
In the space below, write down your thoughts about 2 Corinthians 5:17.

_____

_____

_____

_____

_____

_____

_____

_____

_____

_____

_____

_____

_____

_____

_____

_____

WITH GOD, ALL THINGS ARE POSSIBLE

VERSE 38

But Jesus looked at them and said to them,
"With men this is impossible,
but with God all things are possible."

—

Matthew 19:26 NKJV

Sometimes, because we are imperfect human beings with limited understanding and limited faith, we place limitations on God. But, God's power has no limitations. God will work miracles in our lives if we trust Him with everything we have and everything we are. When we do, we experience the miraculous results of His endless love and His awesome power.

Miracles, both great and small, are an integral part of everyday life, but usually, we are too busy or too cynical to notice God's handiwork. We don't expect to see miracles, so we simply overlook them.

Do you lack the faith that God can work miracles in your own life? If so, it's time to reconsider. If you have allowed yourself to become a "doubting Thomas," you are attempting to place limitations on a God who has none. Instead of doubting your Heavenly Father, you must trust Him. Then, you must wait and watch . . . because something miraculous is going to happen to you, and it might just happen today.

More Great Ideas About Miracles

I have been suspected of being what is called a fundamentalist. That is because I never regard any narrative as unhistorical simply on the ground that it includes the miraculous.

C. S. Lewis

When we face an impossible situation, all self-reliance and self-confidence must melt away; we must be totally dependent on Him for the resources.

Anne Graham Lotz

There is Someone who makes possible what seems completely impossible.

Catherine Marshall

I could go through this day oblivious to the miracles all around me or I could tune in and "enjoy."

Gloria Gaither

Only God can move mountains, but faith and prayer can move God.

E. M. Bounds

Here lies the tremendous mystery—that God should be all-powerful, yet refuse to coerce. He summons us to cooperation. We are honored in being given the opportunity to participate in His good deeds. Remember how He asked for help in performing His miracles: Fill the water pots, stretch out your hand, distribute the loaves.

Elisabeth Elliot

Are you looking for a miracle? If you keep your eyes wide open and trust in God, you won't have to look very far.

Marie T. Freeman

The miracles in fact are a retelling in small letters of the very same story which is written across the whole world in letters too large for some of us to see.

C. S. Lewis

We have a God who delights in impossibilities.

Andrew Murray

Never be afraid to hope—or to ask—for a miracle.

Criswell Freeman

MORE FROM GOD'S WORD

But as it is written: "Eye has not seen, nor ear heard, nor have entered into the heart of man the things which God has prepared for those who love Him."

1 Corinthians 2:9 NKJV

I assure you: The one who believes in Me will also do the works that I do. And he will do even greater works than these, because I am going to the Father.

John 14:12 HCSB

Looking at them, Jesus said, "With men it is impossible, but not with God, because all things are possible with God."

Mark 10:27 HCSB

You are the God who works wonders; You revealed Your strength among the peoples.

Psalm 77:14 HCSB

A TIP

God is in the business of doing miraculous things. You should never be afraid to ask Him for a miracle.

WRITE ABOUT IT:
In the space below, write down your thoughts about God's miraculous power.

_____

_____

_____

_____

_____

_____

_____

_____

_____

_____

_____

_____

_____

_____

_____

_____

VERSE 39

Make a joyful noise unto the LORD,
all ye lands. Serve the LORD with gladness:
come before his presence with singing.

—

Psalm 100:1-2 KJV

When is the best time to "make a joyful noise" by praising God? In church? Before dinner is served? When we tuck little children into bed? None of the above. The best time to praise God is all day, every day, to the greatest extent we can, with thanksgiving in our hearts and with a song on our lips.

Too many of us, even well-intentioned believers, tend to compartmentalize our waking hours into a few familiar categories: work, rest, play, family time, and worship. To do so is a mistake. Worship and praise should be woven into the fabric of everything we do; it should never be relegated to a weekly three-hour visit to church on Sunday morning.

Theologian Wayne Oates once admitted, "Many of my prayers are made with my eyes open. You see, it seems I'm always praying about something, and it's not always convenient—or safe—to close my eyes." Dr. Oates understood that God always hears our prayers and that the relative position of our eyelids is of no concern to Him.

Today, find a little more time to lift your concerns to God in prayer, and praise Him for all that He has done. Whether your eyes are open or closed, He's listening.

MORE GREAT IDEAS ABOUT JOY

Where the soul is full of peace and joy, outward surroundings and circumstances are of comparatively little account.

Hannah Whitall Smith

He wants us to have a faith that does not complain while waiting, but rejoices because we know our times are in His hands—nail-scarred hands that labor for our highest good.

Kay Arthur

Our God is so wonderfully good, and lovely, and blessed in every way that the mere fact of belonging to Him is enough for an untellable fullness of joy!

Hannah Whitall Smith

As Catherine of Siena said, "All the way to heaven is heaven." A joyful end requires a joyful means. Bless the Lord.

Eugene Peterson

When I met Christ,
I felt that I had swallowed
sunshine.

—

E. Stanley Jones

MORE FROM GOD'S WORD

Thou wilt show me the path of life: in thy presence is fulness of joy; at thy right hand there are pleasures for evermore.

Psalm 16:11 KJV

Praise the Lord, all nations! Glorify Him, all peoples! For great is His faithful love to us; the Lord's faithfulness endures forever. Hallelujah!

Psalm 117 HCSB

But I will hope continually and will praise You more and more.

Psalm 71:14 HCSB

Therefore, through Him let us continually offer up to God a sacrifice of praise, that is, the fruit of our lips that confess His name.

Hebrews 13:15 HCSB

A TIP

Joy begins with a choice—the choice to establish a genuine relationship with God and His Son. Joy does not depend upon your circumstances, but upon your relationship with God.

WRITE ABOUT IT:
In the space below, write down your thoughts about the need to praise God every day.

_____

_____

_____

_____

_____

_____

_____

_____

_____

_____

_____

_____

_____

_____

_____

_____

VERSE 40

*Beloved, if God so loved us,
we also ought to love one another.*

—

1 John 4:11 NKJV

Genuine love requires patience and perseverance. Sometimes we are sorely tempted to treat love as if it were a sprint (which it is not). Genuine love is always a marathon, and those who expect it to be otherwise will always be disappointed.

Building lasting relationships requires a steadfast determination to endure, and as an example of perfect perseverance, we need look no further than our Savior, Jesus Christ. Jesus finished what He began. Despite the torture He endured, despite the shame of the cross, Jesus was steadfast in His faithfulness to God. We, too, must remain faithful in our relationships, especially during times of transition or hardship.

The next time you are tempted to "give up" on a relationship, ask yourself this question: "What would our Savior do?" When you find the answer to that question, you will know precisely what you should do.

MORE GREAT IDEAS ABOUT LOVE

The world does not understand theology or dogma, but it does understand love and sympathy.

D. L. Moody

To have fallen in love hints to our hearts that all of earthly life is not hopelessly fallen. Love is the laughter of God.

Beth Moore

For love to be true, it sometimes has to be velvet and sometimes it has to be steel.

Charles Stanley

Real love has staying power. Authentic love is tough love. It refuses to look for ways to run away. It always opts for working through.

Charles Swindoll

So Jesus came, stripping himself of everything as he came—omnipotence, omniscience, omnipresence—everything except love. "He emptied himself" (Philippians 2:7), emptied himself of everything except love. Love—his only protection, his only weapon, his only method.

E. Stanley Jones

Give me such love for God
and men as will blot out
all hatred and bitterness.

—

Dietrich Bonhoeffer

MORE FROM GOD'S WORD

Hatred stirs up conflicts, but love covers all offenses.

Proverbs 10:12 HCSB

And we have this command from Him: the one who loves God must also love his brother.

1 John 4:21 HCSB

Finally, all of you be of one mind, having compassion for one another; love as brothers, be tenderhearted, be courteous.

1 Peter 3:8 NKJV

And be kind and compassionate to one another, forgiving one another, just as God also forgave you in Christ.

Ephesians 4:32 HCSB

Love is patient; love is kind.

1 Corinthians 13:4 HCSB

A TIP

You should love your neighbor as you love yourself. It's a big job, but with God's help, you can do it.

WRITE ABOUT IT:
In the space below, write down your thoughts about 1 John 4:11.

BEYOND GRIEF

VERSE 41

Weeping may endure for a night,
but joy comes in the morning.

—

Psalm 30:5 NKJV

Grief visits all of us who live long and love deeply. When we lose a loved one, or when we experience any other profound loss, darkness overwhelms us for a while, and it seems as if our purpose for living has vanished. Thankfully, God has other plans.

The Christian faith, as communicated through the words of the Holy Bible, is a healing faith. It offers comfort in times of trouble, courage for our fears, hope instead of hopelessness. For Christians, the grave is not a final resting-place, it is a place of transition. Through the healing words of God's promises, Christians understand that the Lord continues to manifest His plan in good times and bad.

God intends that you have a meaningful, abundant life, but He expects you to do your part in claiming those blessings. So, as you work through your grief, you will find it helpful to utilize all the resources that God has placed along your path. God makes help available, but it's up to you to find it and then to accept it.

If you are experiencing the intense pain of a recent loss, or if you are still mourning a loss from long ago, perhaps you are now ready to begin the next stage of your journey with God. If so, be mindful of this fact: As a wounded survivor, you will have countless opportunities to serve others. And by serving others, you will bring purpose and meaning to the suffering you've endured.

MORE GREAT IDEAS ABOUT OVERCOMING GRIEF

You learn your theology most where your sorrows take you.

Martin Luther

God's Word never said we were not to grieve our losses. It says we are not to grieve as those who have no hope (1 Thessalonians 4:13). Big Difference.

Beth Moore

There is no way around suffering. We have to go through it to get to the other side.

Barbara Johnson

Suffering may be someone's fault or it may not be anyone's fault. But if given to God, our suffering becomes an opportunity to experience the power of God at work in our lives and to give glory to Him.

Anne Graham Lotz

Despair is always the gateway of faith.

Oswald Chambers

There is no pit so deep that God's love is not deeper still.

Corrie ten Boom

In times of deepest suffering it is the faithful carrying out of ordinary duties that brings the greatest consolation.

Elisabeth Elliot

The grace of God is sufficient for all our needs, for every problem and for every difficulty, for every broken heart, and for every human sorrow.

Peter Marshall

To pray much is to knock for Him to Whom we pray. This is often done more by groans than speeches, by weeping than by addresses.

St. Augustine

He who becomes a brother to the bruised, a doctor to the despairing, and a comforter to the crushed may not actually say much. What he has to offer is often beyond the power of speech to convey. But, the weary sense it, and it is a balm of Gilead to their souls.

Vance Havner

MORE FROM GOD'S WORD

I have heard your prayer; I have seen your tears. Look, I will heal you.

2 Kings 20:5 HCSB

I called to the Lord in my distress; I called to my God. From His temple He heard my voice.

2 Samuel 22:7 HCSB

Blessed are you who are hungry now, because you will be filled. Blessed are you who weep now, because you will laugh.

Luke 6:21 HCSB

When I sit in darkness, the Lord will be a light to me.

Micah 7:8 NKJV

Lord, how long will You continually forget me? How long will You hide Your face from me?

Psalm 13:1 HCSB

A TIP

When you grieve, God remains steadfast . . . and He can comfort you.

WRITE ABOUT IT:
In the space below, write down your thoughts about Psalm 30:5.

_____

_____

_____

_____

_____

_____

_____

_____

_____

_____

_____

_____

_____

_____

_____

_____

LOVING GOD

VERSE 42

Jesus said to him, "'You shall love the Lord your God with all your heart, with all your soul, and with all your mind.' This is the first and great commandment."

—

Matthew 22:37-38 NKJV

Christ's words are unambiguous: "Love the Lord your God with all your heart and with all your soul and with all your mind." But sometimes, despite our best intentions, we fall short of God's plan for our lives when we become embittered with ourselves, with our neighbors, or most especially with our Creator.

If we are to please God, we must cleanse ourselves of the negative feelings that separate us from others and from Him. In 1 Corinthians 13, we are told that love is the foundation upon which all our relationships are to be built: our relationships with others and our relationship with our Maker.

So today and every day, fill your heart with love; never yield to bitterness; and praise the Son of God who, in His infinite wisdom, made love His greatest commandment.

MORE GREAT IDEAS ABOUT LOVING GOD

I love Him because He first loved me, and He still does love me, and He will love me forever and ever.

Bill Bright

When an honest soul can get still before the living Christ, we can still hear Him say simply and clearly, "Love the Lord your God with all your heart and with all your soul and with all your mind . . . and love one another as I have loved you."

Gloria Gaither

Loving Him means the thankful acceptance of all things that His love has appointed.

Elisabeth Elliot

God is so inconceivably good. He's not looking for perfection. He already saw it in Christ. He's looking for affection.

Beth Moore

God has a genuine, passionate affection for each of us and invites us to open our hearts to that love and then return love to Him with deep sincerity.

Bill Hybels

Joy is a by-product not of happy circumstances, education or talent, but of a healthy relationship with God and a determination to love Him no matter what.

Barbara Johnson

Man was created by God to know and love Him in a permanent, personal relationship.

Anne Graham Lotz

Whatever you love most, be it sports, pleasure, business or God, that is your god.

Billy Graham

In true religion, to love God and to know God are synonymous terms.

C. H. Spurgeon

A man's spiritual health is exactly proportional to his love for God.

C. S. Lewis

MORE FROM GOD'S WORD

This is how we know that we love God's children when we love God and obey His commands.

1 John 5:2 HCSB

Love the Lord your God with all your heart, with all your soul, and with all your strength. These words that I am giving you today are to be in your heart. Repeat them to your children. Talk about them when you sit in your house and when you walk along the road, when you lie down and when you get up.

Deuteronomy 6:5-7 HCSB

And we know that all things work together for good to them that love God, to them who are the called according to his purpose.

Romans 8:28 KJV

Worship the Lord your God and . . . serve Him only.

Matthew 4:10 HCSB

A TIP

Because God first loved you, you should love Him. And one way that you demonstrate your love is by obeying Him.

WRITE ABOUT IT:
In the space below, write down your thoughts about what it means to love God.

_____

_____

_____

_____

_____

_____

_____

_____

_____

_____

_____

_____

_____

_____

_____

ABOVE AND BEYOND FEAR

VERSE 43

Do not fear, for I am with you;
do not be afraid, for I am your God.
I will strengthen you; I will help you;
I will hold on to you with My righteous right hand.

—

Isaiah 41:10 HCSB

We live in a fear-based world, a world where bad new travels at light speed and good news doesn't. These are troubled times, times when we have legitimate fears for the future of our nation, our world, and our families. But we also have every reason to live courageously. After all, since God has promised to love us and protect us, who—or what—should we fear?

Perhaps you, like countless others, have found your courage tested by the anxieties and fears that are an inevitable part of 21st-century life. If so, let the words of Isaiah 41:10 serve as a reminder that God wants you to think less about your challenges and more about His love. Remember that He is not just near, He is here, and He's ready to help right now. God will comfort you if you ask Him to. So why not ask? And why not now?

MORE GREAT IDEAS ABOUT
FEAR

Courage faces fear and thereby masters it. Cowardice represses fear and is thereby mastered by it.

Martin Luther King, Jr.

Whether our fear is absolutely realistic or out of proportion in our minds, our greatest refuge is Jesus Christ.

Luci Swindoll

Only believe, don't fear. Our Master, Jesus, always watches over us, and no matter what the persecution, Jesus will surely overcome it.

Lottie Moon

Fear and doubt are conquered by a faith that rejoices. And faith can rejoice because the promises of God are as certain as God Himself.

Kay Arthur

Are you fearful? First, bow your head and pray for God's strength. Then, raise your head and look Old Man Trouble squarely in the eye. Chances are, Old Man Trouble will blink.

Jim Gallery

When once we are assured that God is good, then there can be nothing left to fear.

Hannah Whitall Smith

Our future may look fearfully intimidating, yet we can look up to the Engineer of the Universe, confident that nothing escapes His attention or slips out of the control of those strong hands.

Elisabeth Elliot

Earthly fears are no fears at all. Answer the big question of eternity, and the little questions of life fall into perspective.

Max Lucado

There is not only fear, but terrible danger, for the life unguarded by God.

Oswald Chambers

The Bible is a Christian's guidebook, and I believe the knowledge it sheds on pain and suffering is the great antidote to fear for suffering people. Knowledge can dissolve fear as light destroys darkness.

Philip Yancey

MORE FROM GOD'S WORD

Don't be afraid. Only believe.

Mark 5:36 HCSB

Even when I go through the darkest valley, I fear [no] danger, for You are with me.

Psalm 23:4 HCSB

I sought the Lord, and He heard me, and delivered me from all my fears.

Psalm 34:4 NKJV

Do not fear, for I am with you; do not be afraid, for I am your God. I will strengthen you; I will help you; I will hold on to you with My righteous right hand.

Isaiah 41:10 HCSB

Indeed, God is my salvation. I will trust [Him] and not be afraid.

Isaiah 12:2 HCSB

A TIP

Are you feeling anxious or fearful? If so, trust God to handle those problems that are simply too big for you to solve. Entrust the future—your future—to God.

WRITE ABOUT IT:
In the space below, write down your thoughts about Isaiah 41:10.

GOD'S MERCY

VERSE 44

The LORD is gracious and full of compassion,
slow to anger and great in mercy.
The LORD is good to all,
and His tender mercies are over all His works.

—

Psalm 145:8-9 NKJV

In Psalm 145, we are taught that God is merciful. His hand offers forgiveness and salvation. God's mercy, like His love, is infinite and everlasting—it knows no boundaries.

Romans 3:23 reminds us of a universal truth: "All have sinned, and come short of the glory of God" (KJV). All of us, even the most righteous among us, are sinners. But despite our imperfections, our merciful Father in heaven offers us salvation through the person of His Son.

As Christians, we have been blessed by a merciful, loving God. Now, it's our turn to share His love and His mercy with a world that needs both. May we accept His gifts and share them with our friends, with our families, and with all the people He chooses to place along our paths.

MORE GREAT IDEAS ABOUT GOD'S MERCY

Mercy is an attribute of God, an infinite and inexhaustible energy within the divine nature which disposes God to be actively compassionate.

A. W. Tozer

How happy we are when we realize that He is responsible, that He goes before, that goodness and mercy shall follow us!

Mrs. Charles E. Cowman

Is your child learning of the love of God through your love, tenderness, and mercy?

James Dobson

Trust the past to the mercy of God, the present to his love, and the future to his Providence.

St. Augustine

We must appropriate the tender mercy of God every day after conversion, or problems quickly develop. We need his grace daily in order to live a righteous life.

Jim Cymbala

When terrible things happen, there are two choices, and only two: We can trust God, or we can defy Him. We believe that God is God, He's still got the whole world in His hands and knows exactly what He's doing, or we must believe that He is not God and that we are at the awful mercy of mere chance.

Elisabeth Elliot

Looking back over my life, all I can see is mercy and grace written in large letters everywhere. May God help me have the same kind of heart toward those who wound or offend me.

Jim Cymbala

The Creator has given to us the awesome responsibility of representing him to our children. Our heavenly Father is a God of unlimited love, and our children must become acquainted with his mercy and tenderness through our own love toward them.

James Dobson

Storm the throne of grace and persevere therein, and mercy will come down.

John Wesley

MORE FROM GOD'S WORD

Help me, O Lord my God! Oh, save me according to Your mercy.

Psalm 109:26 NKJV

He has shown you, O man, what is good; And what does the LORD require of you but to do justly, to love mercy, and to walk humbly with your God?

Micah 6:8 NKJV

See, we count as blessed those who have endured. You have heard of Job's endurance and have seen the outcome from the Lord: the Lord is very compassionate and merciful.

James 5:11 HCSB

But God, who is abundant in mercy, because of His great love that He had for us, made us alive with the Messiah even though we were dead in trespasses. By grace you are saved!

Ephesians 2:4-5 HCSB

A TIP

God forgives sin when you ask . . . so ask! God stands ready to forgive . . . the next move is yours.

WRITE ABOUT IT:
In the space below, write down your thoughts about God's mercy.

_____

_____

_____

_____

_____

_____

_____

_____

_____

_____

_____

_____

_____

_____

_____

_____

_____

_____

VERSE 45

Blessed is the man who walks not in the counsel
of the ungodly, nor stands in the path of sinners,
nor sits in the seat of the scornful;
but his delight is in the law of the Lord,
and in His law he meditates day and night.

—

Psalm 1:1-2 NKJV

Peer pressure can be a good thing or a bad thing, depending upon your peers. If your peers encourage you to make integrity a habit—and if they encourage you to follow God's will and to obey His commandments—then you'll experience positive peer pressure, and that's good. But, if you are involved with people who encourage you to do foolish things, you're facing a different kind of peer pressure . . . and you'd better beware. When you feel pressured to do things, or to say things, that lead you away from God, you're aiming straight for trouble.

Are you satisfied to follow that crowd? If so, you may pay a heavy price unless you've picked the right crowd. And while you're deciding whom to follow, be sure you're determined to follow the One from Galilee, too. Jesus will guide your steps and bless your undertakings if you let Him. Your challenge, of course, is to let Him.

To sum it up, here's your choice: you can choose to please God first (and by doing so, strengthen your character), or you can fall prey to peer pressure. The choice is yours—and so are the consequences.

MORE GREAT IDEAS ABOUT
PEER PRESSURE

It is comfortable to know that we are responsible to God and not to man. It is a small matter to be judged of man's judgement.

Lottie Moon

We, as God's people, are not only to stay far away from sin and sinners who would entice us, but we are to be so like our God that we mourn over sin.

Kay Arthur

You will get untold flak for prioritizing God's revealed and present will for your life over man's . . . but, boy, is it worth it.

Beth Moore

Comparison is the root of all feelings of inferiority.

James Dobson

For better or worse, you will eventually become more and more like the people you associate with. So why not associate with people who make you better, not worse?

Marie T. Freeman

It is impossible to please God doing things motivated by and produced by the flesh.

—

Bill Bright

MORE FROM GOD'S WORD

He who walks with wise men will be wise, but the companion of fools will be destroyed.

Proverbs 13:20 NKJV

Do not be deceived: "Bad company corrupts good morals."

1 Corinthians 15:33 HCSB

For am I now trying to win the favor of people, or God? Or am I striving to please people? If I were still trying to please people, I would not be a slave of Christ.

Galatians 1:10 HCSB

Stay away from a foolish man; you will gain no knowledge from his speech.

Proverbs 14:7 HCSB

A TIP

Your world is loaded up with pressures, some good and some bad. Your big challenge is to know the difference and act accordingly.

WRITE ABOUT IT:

In the space below, write down your thoughts about the pressure to keep up with the Joneses.

_____

_____

_____

_____

_____

_____

_____

_____

_____

_____

_____

_____

_____

_____

_____

_____

_____

VERSE 46

*Even though I walk through the valley
of the shadow of death,
I will fear no evil, for you are with me;
your rod and your staff, they comfort me.*

—

Psalm 23:4 NIV

In the 23rd Psalm, David teaches us that God is like a watchful Shepherd caring for His flock. No wonder these verses have provided comfort and hope for generations of believers.

You are precious in the eyes of God. You are His priceless creation, made in His image, and protected by Him. God watches over every step you make and every breath you take, so you need never be afraid. But sometimes, fear has a way of slipping into the minds and hearts of even the most devout believers—and you are no exception.

You know from firsthand experience that life is not always easy. But as a recipient of God's grace, you also know that you are protected by a loving Heavenly Father.

On occasion, you will confront circumstances that trouble you to the very core of your soul. When you are afraid, trust in God. When you are worried, turn your concerns over to Him. When you are anxious, be still and listen for the quiet assurance of God's promises. And then, place your life in His hands. He is your Shepherd today and throughout eternity. Trust the Shepherd.

MORE GREAT IDEAS ABOUT GOD'S COMFORT

When I am criticized, injured, or afraid, there is a Father who is ready to comfort me.

Max Lucado

Put your hand into the hand of God. He gives the calmness and serenity of heart and soul.

Mrs. Charles E. Cowman

When God allows extraordinary trials for His people, He prepares extraordinary comforts for them.

Corrie ten Boom

The God of the galaxies is the God who knows when your heart is broken—and He can heal it!

Warren Wiersbe

You don't have to be alone in your hurt! Comfort is yours. Joy is an option. And it's all been made possible by your Savior. He went without comfort so you might have it. He postponed joy so you might share in it. He willingly chose isolation so you might never be alone in your hurt and sorrow.

Joni Eareckson Tada

To know that God rules over all—that there are no accidents in life, that no tactic of Satan or man can ever thwart the will of God—brings divine comfort.

Kay Arthur

Pour out your heart to God and tell Him how you feel. Be real, be honest, and when you get it all out, you'll start to feel the gradual covering of God's comforting presence.

Bill Hybels

God's promises are medicine for the broken heart. Let Him comfort you. And, after He has comforted you, try to share that comfort with somebody else. It will do both of you good.

Warren Wiersbe

My prayer for you today is that you will feel the loving arms of God wrapped around you.

Billy Graham

We all go through pain and sorrow, but the presence of God, like a warm, comforting blanket, can shield us and protect us, and allow the deep inner joy to surface, even in the most devastating circumstances.

Barbara Johnson

MORE FROM GOD'S WORD

The Lord is gracious and compassionate, slow to anger and great in faithful love. The Lord is good to everyone; His compassion [rests] on all He has made.

Psalm 145:8-9 HCSB

God is faithful, by whom you were called into the fellowship of His Son, Jesus Christ our Lord.

1 Corinthians 1:9 NKJV

Those who trust in the Lord are like Mount Zion. It cannot be shaken; it remains forever.

Psalm 125:1 HCSB

I will be with you when you pass through the waters . . . when you walk through the fire . . . the flame will not burn you. For I the Lord your God, the Holy One of Israel, and your Savior.

Isaiah 43:2-3 HCSB

A TIP

God will always comfort you so that you, in turn, can have the strength to comfort others.

Write About It:

In the space below, write down your thoughts about God's comfort.

_____

_____

_____

_____

_____

_____

_____

_____

_____

_____

_____

_____

_____

_____

_____

_____

VERSE 47

God is our refuge and strength,
a very present help in trouble.

—

Psalm 46:1 NKJV

The words of Psalm 46:1 promise that God is our refuge, a refuge that we all need. From time to time, all of us face adversity, discouragement, or disappointment. And throughout life, we all must endure life-changing personal losses that leave us breathless. When we do, God stands ready to protect us. Psalm 147 assures us that, "He heals the brokenhearted, and binds their wounds" (v. 3, NIV).

Are you anxious? Take those anxieties to God. Are you troubled? Take your troubles to Him. Does the world seem to be trembling beneath your feet? Seek protection from the One who cannot be moved.

The same God who created the universe stands ready and willing to comfort you and to restore your strength. During life's most difficult days, your Heavenly Father remains steadfast. And, in His own time and according to His master plan, He will heal you if you invite Him into your heart.

MORE GREAT IDEAS ABOUT TOUGH TIMES

The sermon of your life in tough times ministers to people more powerfully than the most eloquent speaker.

Bill Bright

Faith is a strong power, mastering any difficulty in the strength of the Lord who made heaven and earth.

Corrie ten Boom

If all struggles and sufferings were eliminated, the spirit would no more reach maturity than would the child.

Elisabeth Elliot

God will never let you sink under your circumstances. He always provides a safety net and His love always encircles.

Barbara Johnson

Sometimes we get tired of the burdens of life, but we know that Jesus Christ will meet us at the end of life's journey. And, that makes all the difference.

Billy Graham

Measure the size of the obstacles against the size of God.

Beth Moore

Even in the winter, even in the midst of the storm, the sun is still there. Somewhere, up above the clouds, it still shines and warms and pulls at the life buried deep inside the brown branches and frozen earth. The sun is there! Spring will come.

Gloria Gaither

God allows us to experience the low points of life in order to teach us lessons that we could learn in no other way.

C. S. Lewis

Our loving God uses difficulty in our lives to burn away the sin of self and build faith and spiritual power.

Bill Bright

Adversity is always unexpected and unwelcomed. It is an intruder and a thief, and yet in the hands of God, adversity becomes the means through which His supernatural power is demonstrated.

Charles Swindoll

MORE FROM GOD'S WORD

Consider it a great joy, my brothers, whenever you experience various trials, knowing that the testing of your faith produces endurance. But endurance must do its complete work, so that you may be mature and complete, lacking nothing.

James 1:2-4 HCSB

When you are in distress and all these things have happened to you, you will return to the Lord your God in later days and obey Him. He will not leave you, destroy you, or forget the covenant with your fathers that He swore to them by oath, because the Lord your God is a compassionate God.

Deuteronomy 4:30-31 HCSB

Whatever has been born of God conquers the world. This is the victory that has conquered the world: our faith.

1 John 5:4 HCSB

A TIP

When you experience tough times (and you will), a positive attitude makes a big difference in the way you tackle your problems.

Write About It:
In the space below, write down your thoughts about Psalm 46:1.

_____

_____

_____

_____

_____

_____

_____

_____

_____

_____

_____

_____

_____

_____

_____

_____

_____

HE WATCHES OVER US

VERSE 48

Unless the Lord builds a house,
its builders labor over it in vain;
unless the Lord watches over a city,
the watchman stays alert in vain.

—

Psalm 127:1 HCSB

Have you ever faced challenges that seemed too big to handle? Have you ever faced big problems that, despite your best efforts, simply could not be solved? If so, you know how uncomfortable it is to feel helpless in the face of difficult circumstances. Thankfully, even when there's nowhere else to turn, you can turn your thoughts and prayers to God, and He will respond.

God's hand uplifts those who turn their hearts and prayers to Him. Count yourself among that number. When you do, you can live courageously and joyfully, knowing that "this too will pass"—but that God's love for you will not. And you can draw strength from the knowledge that you are a marvelous creation, loved, protected, and uplifted by the ever-present hand of God.

More Great Ideas About God's Protection

When you fall and skin your knees and skin your heart, He'll pick you up.

Charles Stanley

In all the old castles of England, there was a place called the keep. It was always the strongest and best protected place in the castle, and in it were hidden all who were weak and helpless and unable to defend themselves in times of danger. Shall we be afraid to hide ourselves in the keeping power of our Divine Keeper, who neither slumbers nor sleeps, and who has promised to preserve our going out and our coming in, from this time forth and even forever more?

Hannah Whitall Smith

Trials are not enemies of faith but opportunities to reveal God's faithfulness.

Barbara Johnson

Our future may look fearfully intimidating, yet we can look up to the Engineer of the Universe, confident that nothing escapes His attention or slips out of the control of those strong hands.

Elisabeth Elliot

Through all of the crises of life—and we all are going to experience them—we have this magnificent Anchor.

Franklin Graham

My case is urgent, and I do not see how I am to be delivered; but this is no business of mine. He who makes the promise will find ways and means of keeping it. It is mine to obey His command; it is not mine to direct His counsels. I am His servant, not His solicitor. I call upon Him, and He will deliver.

C. H. Spurgeon

God delights in spreading His protective wings and enfolding His frightened, weary, beaten-down, worn-out children.

Bill Hybels

There is no safer place to live than the center of His will.

Calvin Miller

Gather the riches of God's promises which can strengthen you in the time when there will be no freedom.

Corrie ten Boom

MORE FROM GOD'S WORD

The Lord bless you and protect you; the Lord make His face shine on you, and be gracious to you.

Numbers 6:24-25 HCSB

You are the God who works wonders; You revealed Your strength among the peoples.

Psalm 77:14 HCSB

Ah, Lord God! Behold, You have made the heavens and the earth by Your great power and outstretched arm. There is nothing too hard for You.

Jeremiah 32:17 NKJV

But the Lord will be a refuge for His people.

Joel 3:16 HCSB

A TIP

When you are in the center of God's will, you are in the center of God's protection.

WRITE ABOUT IT:
In the space below, write down your thoughts
about God's protection.

_____

_____

_____

_____

_____

_____

_____

_____

_____

_____

_____

_____

_____

_____

_____

_____

_____

_____

VERSE 49

Love is patient; love is kind.
Love does not envy; is not boastful;
is not conceited; does not act improperly;
is not selfish; is not provoked;
does not keep a record of wrongs;
finds no joy in unrighteousness,
but rejoices in the truth;
bears all things, believes all things,
hopes all things, endures all things.

—

1 Corinthians 13:4-7 HCSB

Love is a choice. Either you choose to behave lovingly toward others . . . or not; either you behave yourself in ways that enhance your relationships . . . or not. But make no mistake: genuine love requires effort. Simply put, if you wish to build lasting relationships, you must be willing to do your part.

Since the days of Adam and Eve, God has allowed His children to make choices for themselves, and so it is with you. As you interact with family and friends, you have choices to make . . . lots of them. If you choose wisely, you'll be rewarded; if you choose unwisely, you'll bear the consequences.

God does not intend for you to experience mediocre relationships; He created you for far greater things. Building lasting relationships requires compassion, wisdom, empathy, kindness, courtesy, and forgiveness (lots of forgiveness). If that sounds a lot like work, it is—which is perfectly fine with God. Why? Because He knows that you are capable of doing that work, and because He knows that the fruits of your labors will enrich the lives of your loved ones and the lives of generations yet unborn.

MORE GREAT IDEAS ABOUT LOVE

It is important to know that you have to work to keep love alive; you have to protect it and maintain it, just like you would a delicate flower.

James Dobson

How do you spell love? When you reach the point where the happiness, security, and development of another person is as much of a driving force to you as your own happiness, security, and development, then you have a mature love. True love is spelled G-I-V-E. It is not based on what you can get, but rooted in what you can give to the other person.

Josh McDowell

The truth of the Gospel is intended to free us to love God and others with our whole heart.

John Eldredge

Truth becomes hard if it is not softened by love, and love becomes soft if not strengthened by truth.

E. Stanley Jones

Love is a steady wish for the loved person's ultimate good.

C. S. Lewis

*Beloved, if God so loved us,
we also ought to love one another.*

—

1 John 4:11 NASB

MORE FROM GOD'S WORD

I pray that you, being rooted and firmly established in love, may be able to comprehend with all the saints what is the breadth and width, height and depth, and to know the Messiah's love that surpasses knowledge, so you may be filled with all the fullness of God.

Ephesians 3:17-19 HCSB

Dear friend, you are showing your faith by whatever you do for the brothers, and this you are doing for strangers.

3 John 1:5 HCSB

In every way I've shown you that by laboring like this, it is necessary to help the weak and to keep in mind the words of the Lord Jesus, for He said, "It is more blessed to give than to receive."

Acts 20:35 HCSB

A TIP

The key to successful Christian living lies in your submission to the Spirit of God. If you're a Christian, God has commanded you to love people . . . and it's a commandment that covers both saints and sinners.

WRITE ABOUT IT:
In the space below, write down your thoughts
about 1 Corinthians 13:4-7.

_____

_____

_____

_____

_____

_____

_____

_____

_____

_____

_____

_____

_____

_____

_____

_____

MOUNTAIN-MOVING FAITH

VERSE 50

*If you have faith as a mustard seed,
you will say to this mountain,
"Move from here to there,"
and it will move;
and nothing will be impossible for you.*

—

Matthew 17:20 NKJV

Because we live in a demanding world, all of us have mountains to climb and mountains to move. Moving those mountains requires faith.

Are you a mountain mover whose faith is evident for all to see? Or, are you a spiritual shrinking violet? God needs more men and women who are willing to move mountains for His glory and for His kingdom.

Jesus taught His disciples that if they had faith, they could move mountains. You can too. When you place your faith, your trust, indeed your life in the hands of Christ Jesus, you'll be amazed at the marvelous things He can do. So strengthen your faith through praise, through worship, through Bible study, and through prayer. And trust God's plans. With Him, all things are possible, and He stands ready to open a world of possibilities to you . . . if you have faith.

Concentration camp survivor Corrie ten Boom relied on faith during her long months of imprisonment and torture. Later, despite the fact that four of her family members had died in Nazi death camps, Corrie's faith was unshaken. She wrote, "There is no pit so deep that God's love is not deeper still." Christians take note: Genuine faith in God means faith in all circumstances, happy or sad, joyful or tragic.

If your faith is being tested to the point of breaking, remember that your Savior is near. If you reach out to Him in faith, He will give you peace and strength. Reach out today. If you touch even the smallest fragment of the Master's garment, He will make you whole. And then, with no further ado, let the mountain moving begin.

MORE GREAT IDEAS ABOUT FAITH

There are a lot of things in life that are difficult to understand. Faith allows the soul to go beyond what the eyes can see.

John Maxwell

Faith is seeing light with the eyes of your heart, when the eyes of your body see only darkness.

Barbara Johnson

Just as our faith strengthens our prayer life, so do our prayers deepen our faith. Let us pray often, starting today, for a deeper, more powerful faith.

Shirley Dobson

The popular idea of faith is of a certain obstinate optimism: the hope, tenaciously held in the face of trouble, that the universe is fundamentally friendly and things may get better.

J. I. Packer

Faith does not concern itself with the entire journey. One step is enough.

Mrs. Charles E. Cowman

If God chooses to remain silent, faith is content.

Ruth Bell Graham

I am truly grateful that faith enables me to move past the question of "Why?"

Zig Ziglar

When you enroll in the "school of faith," you never know what may happen next. The life of faith presents challenges that keep you going—and keep you growing!

Warren Wiersbe

Nothing is more disastrous than to study faith, analyze faith, make noble resolves of faith, but never actually to make the leap of faith.

Vance Havner

Grace calls you to get up, throw off your blanket of helplessness, and to move on through life in faith.

Kay Arthur

MORE FROM GOD'S WORD

For we walk by faith, not by sight.

2 Corinthians 5:7 HCSB

Now faith is the reality of what is hoped for, the proof of what is not seen.

Hebrews 11:1 HCSB

Now without faith it is impossible to please God, for the one who draws near to Him must believe that He exists and rewards those who seek Him.

Hebrews 11:6 HCSB

If you do not stand firm in your faith, then you will not stand at all.

Isaiah 7:9 HCSB

Jesus said, "Because you have seen Me, you have believed. Blessed are those who believe without seeing."

John 20:29 HCSB

A TIP

If your faith is strong enough, you and God—working together—can move mountains.

WRITE ABOUT IT:
In the space below, write down your thoughts about Matthew 17:20.

_____

_____

_____

_____

_____

_____

_____

_____

_____

_____

_____

_____

_____

_____

_____

_____

_____

VERSE 51

So teach us to number our days,
that we may gain a heart of wisdom.

—

Psalm 90:12 NKJV

Life is a glorious gift from God. Treat it that way. This day, like every other, is filled to the brim with opportunities, challenges, and choices. But, no choice that you make is more important than the choice you make concerning God. Today, you will either place Him at the center of your life—or not—and the consequences of that choice have implications that are both temporal and eternal.

Sometimes, we don't intentionally neglect God; we simply allow ourselves to become overwhelmed with the demands of everyday life. And then, without our even realizing it, we gradually drift away from the One we need most. Thankfully, God never drifts away from us. He remains always present, always steadfast, always loving.

As you begin this day, place God and His Son where they belong: in your head, in your prayers, on your lips, and in your heart. And then, with God as your guide and companion, let the journey begin . . .

MORE GREAT IDEAS ABOUT LIFE

Jesus wants Life for us, Life with a capital L.

John Eldredge

You have a glorious future in Christ! Live every moment in His power and love.

Vonette Bright

As I contemplate all the sacrifices required in order to live a life that is totally focused on Jesus Christ and His eternal kingdom, the joy seeps out of my heart onto my face in a smile of deep satisfaction.

Anne Graham Lotz

Your life is not a boring stretch of highway. It's a straight line to heaven. And just look at the fields ripening along the way. Look at the tenacity and endurance. Look at the grains of righteousness. You'll have quite a crop at harvest . . . so don't give up!

Joni Eareckson Tada

The value of a life can only be estimated by its relationship to God.

Oswald Chambers

The world has never been stable. Jesus Himself was born into the cruelest and most unstable of worlds. No, we have babies and keep trusting and living because the Resurrection is true! The Resurrection was not just a one-time event in history; it is a principle built into the very fabric of our beings, a fact reverberating from every cell of creation: Life wins! Life wins!

Gloria Gaither

A life lived without reflection can be very superficial and empty.

Elisabeth Elliot

The whole point of this life is the healing of the heart's eye through which God is seen.

St. Augustine

Life is a gift from God, and we must treasure it, protect it, and invest it.

Warren Wiersbe

Our Lord is the Bread of Life. His proportions are perfect. There never was too much or too little of anything about Him. Feed on Him for a well-balanced ration. All the vitamins and calories are there.

Vance Havner

MORE FROM GOD'S WORD

Jesus told him, "I am the way, the truth, and the life. No one comes to the Father except through Me."

John 14:6 HCSB

I urge you now to live the life to which God called you.

Ephesians 4:1 NKJV

Shout triumphantly to the Lord, all the earth. Serve the Lord with gladness; come before Him with joyful songs.

Psalm 100:1-2 HCSB

I have set before you life and death, blessing and curse. Choose life so that you and your descendants may live, love the Lord your God, obey Him, and remain faithful to Him. For He is your life, and He will prolong your life in the land the Lord swore to give to your fathers Abraham, Isaac, and Jacob.

Deuteronomy 30:19-20 HCSB

A TIP

Your life is a priceless opportunity, a gift of incalculable worth. You should thank God for the gift of life . . . and you should use that gift wisely.

WRITE ABOUT IT:
In the space below, write down your thoughts about Psalm 90:12.

_____

_____

_____

_____

_____

_____

_____

_____

_____

_____

_____

_____

_____

_____

_____

_____

_____

_____

VERSE 52

*Go, therefore, and make disciples of all nations,
baptizing them in the name of the Father
and of the Son and of the Holy Spirit,
teaching them to observe
everything I have commanded you.
And remember, I am with you always,
to the end of the age.*

—

Matthew 28:19-20 HCSB

Are you a bashful Christian, one who is afraid to speak up for your Savior. Do you leave it up to others to share their testimonies while you stand on the sidelines, reluctant to share yours? Too many of us are slow to obey the last commandment of the risen Christ; we don't do our best to "make disciples of all the nations."

Christ's Great Commission applies to Christians of every generation, including our own. As believers, we are commanded to share the Good News with our families, with our neighbors, and with the world. Jesus invited His disciples to become fishers of men. We, too, must accept the Savior's invitation, and we must do so today. Tomorrow may indeed be too late.

MORE GREAT IDEAS ABOUT
THE GREAT COMMISSION

You cannot keep silent once you have experienced salvation of Jesus Christ.

Warren Wiersbe

Our commission is quite specific. We are told to be His witness to all nations. For us, as His disciples, to refuse any part of this commission frustrates the love of Jesus Christ, the Son of God.

Catherine Marshall

There are many timid souls whom we jostle morning and evening as we pass them by; but if only the kind word were spoken they might become fully persuaded.

Fanny Crosby

Your light is the truth of the Gospel message itself as well as your witness as to Who Jesus is and what He has done for you. Don't hide it.

Anne Graham Lotz

To stand in an uncaring world and say, "See, here is the Christ" is a daring act of courage.

Calvin Miller

How many people have you made homesick for God?

Oswald Chambers

There is nothing anybody else can do that can stop God from using us. We can turn everything into a testimony.

Corrie ten Boom

Choose Jesus Christ! Deny yourself, take up the Cross, and follow Him—for the world must be shown. The world must see, in us, a discernible, visible, startling difference.

Elisabeth Elliot

There is nothing more appealing or convincing to a watching world than to hear the testimony of someone who has just been with Jesus.

Henry Blackaby

If we are ever going to be or do anything for our Lord, now is the time.

Vance Havner

MORE FROM GOD'S WORD

But you will receive power when the Holy Spirit has come upon you, and you will be My witnesses in Jerusalem, in all Judea and Samaria, and to the ends of the earth.

Acts 1:8 HCSB

Now then we are ambassadors for Christ . . . .

2 Corinthians 5:20 KJV

And I say to you, anyone who acknowledges Me before men, the Son of Man will also acknowledge him before the angels of God; but whoever denies Me before men will be denied before the angels of God.

Luke 12:8-9 HCSB

You are the light of the world. A city that is set on a hill cannot be hidden. Nor do they light a lamp and put it under a basket, but on a lampstand, and it gives light to all who are in the house. Let your light so shine before men, that they may see your good works and glorify your Father in heaven.

Matthew 5:14–16 NKJV

A TIP

The best day to respond to Christ's Great Commission is this day.

WRITE ABOUT IT:
In the space below, write down your thoughts about the Great Commission.

_____

_____

_____

_____

_____

_____

_____

_____

_____

_____

_____

_____

_____

_____

_____

_____

_____